Denver Museum of Natural History
and
Roberts Rinehart Publishers

Mountain *lion*

PUMA

PANTHER

PAINTER

COUGAR

Written by
Sandra Chisholm Robinson

Designed and Illustrated by
Ann W. Douden
and
Gail Kohler Opsahl

The author thanks the following people for reviewing *Mountain Lion*: from Yellowstone National Park, George Robinson, Chief Naturalist; and from the Wildlife Research Institute, Dr. Maurice Hornocker and Researcher Kerry Murphy. For their critique of the story, special thanks to Greg Kroll, Yellowstone National Park District Naturalist; Paul Schullery, Yellowstone Research writer/editor; Spanish teacher Deborah J. Olig from the Gardiner School, Gardiner, Montana; and the students and their teacher, Kim Willson, of Gardiner's third-grade class. Librarian Kathryn Branaugh was very helpful in locating resources. Mountain lion researcher Kerry Murphy and his staff were very generous in providing information and photographs for this project. And thanks to my son, Garrett, whose imagination and honesty are a real inspiration to his mom.

Published by Roberts Rinehart Publishers
Post Office Box 666, Niwot, Colorado 80544-0666

Library of Congress Catalog Card Number 91-60433-1
International Standard Book Number 1-879373-07-6

Manufactured in the United States of America

Mountain lion

CONTENTS

INTRODUCTION

"*El Encanto*" (the Enchantment) is an allegory, a story with more than one meaning. The setting is Mexico and the time is the early 1900s. However, the setting could be almost anywhere in the world and the time could be now. This fable is about the changes that people can make in their environment and how these changes affect the quality of their lives.

On one level, this is the story of a small, struggling farming village. Though poor in substance, the community is rich in character. The young girl, María, a loving but determined individual, does not allow others to make her choices for her. The kind and humble Don Miguel searches for wisdom in distant places when the answers are always close to home.

This is also the story of *el león*, the mountain lion. The Spanish term *el encanto* means enchantment, charm, fascination, or delight. This story tells of the enchantment that wild animals and wild places bring to our lives.

The story "*El Encanto*" and the information and activities that follow will provide children and parents, students and teachers, and wildlife enthusiasts with several views of the elusive mountain lion — the gentle mother who nourishes her young and diligently trains them to survive alone; the skilled hunter, revered by Native American tribes, that kills prey often larger and faster than itself; the opportunist stalking deer on the manicured lawns and plazas of western cities, sometimes threatening pets and even people.

Can we learn to live with the mountain lion and other wild creatures? If we can, then the enchantment is ours.

El Encanto

(the enchantment)

I GREW UP IN A SMALL VILLAGE
with my mother, father, and brothers. My brothers worked in the fields with my father and herded our small flock of sheep. Rising long before the sun, Mother was busy at the metate (grinding stone) grinding the corn for the breakfast and noon tortillas.

I helped my mother serve the simple breakfast of cinnamon tea, beans, tortillas, and chile sauce. When I look around at all the things people have today, I sometimes think that I was poor as a child. But I was not poor. My family's love warmed me when I was cold, and cheered me when I was sad.

Our white adobe house, with bright red chiles hanging from the roof, had two rooms — the main room and the kitchen. The door from the main room opened onto my mother's garden. As the sun warmed the air, the sweet perfume of my mother's flowers filled our tiny home. My mother and I sprinkled and swept the hard dirt floors, and kept the house clean inside and out. But we could not keep the flies away.

My father worked hard and was a good-humored man. Sometimes I would sit quietly in his lap. He would stroke my long, black hair and call me his beautiful ángelita (little angel). Today I am a wrinkled old woman, and still I feel very beautiful. But my story is from yesterday, when I was a little girl. . . .

"HURRY, MARIA,
I have fresh flowers from my garden for Don Miguel."
María's mother, Señora Medina, wrapped her shawl around
her head and shoulders.

"I'm coming, *Mamá*." The small girl skipped through the
doorway into the garden.

Señora Medina sighed and smiled. After six sons, the saints
had blessed her with a beautiful daughter. The child's long,
black hair glistened in the sunlight, and her dark eyes
reflected great love and intelligence.

However, remembering yesterday's events, Señora Medina's
smile faded. When her neighbor, Doña Carmelita, collared a
small dog for chasing the chickens in her yard, she began
to beat it with a stick. Doña Carmelita was known for her hot
temper! The poor puppy had cried pitifully. The villagers
turned away because it was not their business. María,
hearing the animal's cries, and understanding that the
grown-ups were not going to help, took matters into her own
hands. Grabbing a stick of firewood, she ran toward Doña
Carmelita, who was still bent over the whimpering puppy.
Taking aim, María struck the large rump of Doña Carmelita
with the stick. More surprised than hurt, Doña Carmelita
released the dog, who gratefully jumped into María's arms.
Don Miguel, who was like a *padrino* (godfather) to María,
whisked the girl and dog away before Doña Carmelita could
unleash her fury on the pair.

Señora Medina's heart felt warm when she thought of Don
Miguel. The man lived alone in a tiny house outside the
village. The señora knew that he had the wealth to live in a
finer home, but he did not wish to arouse the envy of his
neighbors. Don Miguel was a wise and humble man. His
small house was filled with books. Unlike most of the
villagers, he could even read the words in those books!

When María was just a baby her father, Don José, had fallen
ill. Doña Magdalena, the *curandera* (curer), had prayed,
brushed him with herbs, and passed an unbroken egg over
him to draw out and trap the evil airs. While Don José lay ill,
the corn ripened in the fields. By harvest time, Don José
was better, but still too sick to rise from his bed. His sons
were too little to work the fields alone. The family would
starve if they could not harvest the corn. Señora Medina
prayed before the rough wooden altar in her home. The next
morning Don Miguel arrived at her door, collected the boys,
and harvested the corn.

There was much gossip about Don Miguel in the tiny village. After overhearing the village women, María had breathlessly asked him, "Were you really a *vaquero* (cowboy)? Is it true that you lived with Indians, and rode with Billy the Kid?"

The man had only laughed and said, "Dress a monkey as you will, it remains a monkey still."

The mother and daughter walked briskly to the village plaza. It was busy at the market place as the women bought food for the day's meals. Suddenly María saw Don Miguel and, running to him, pressed the flowers into his arms.

The old man said to Señora Medina, "You are too generous." Turning to María he said, "And I have a present for you." From his pocket he removed a small statue. The figure wore long robes and the face, though roughly carved, was beautiful. "Saint Francis,* María. You share his love of animals. And after the beating you gave Doña Carmelita, I believe you share his courage, too." Don Miguel winked at the dark-eyed child.

María's mother gently scolded him, "Do not encourage her, Don Miguel. . . ."

But Señora Medina stopped abruptly. Loud, angry voices rose from the market place. Don Ignacio, who owned the largest herd of sheep in the village, had gathered a large group of men who had come in from the fields.

"Last night, *el león* (mountain lion) killed one of my sheep. We are a poor people. We cannot afford these losses. I say we hunt down the beast that steals from us."

Don Ignacio went on, "We will drive the mountain lions, bears, and wolves from our valley and the mountains that surround it."

María's father, Don José, spoke up. "*El león* takes just a little. Perhaps we should be more vigilant in watching our sheep." Don José winked at his companion. "Greed tears a man's sack, Don Ignacio."

Some of the villagers laughed.

* Saint Francis was a real man born in 1182 in Italy. Because of his ideas about wild animals and people's relationships with the environment, modern philosophers have proposed him as the patron saint of ecology.

"Perhaps I can help." A short man in long, rough robes with a rope tied at his waist stepped from a grove of cottonwood trees that bordered one side of the plaza. Grasping the callused hand of Don Miguel, María gazed in wonder at the stranger. With his dark hair and eyes, and skin the rich, deep color of the earth, he looked much like the people that the child had known all her life. But the stranger's eyes seemed to hold the sadness and happiness lived by a man of a thousand years — eyes that knew what a person was before that person said a word. María looked away; she had been thinking some very bad thoughts about Doña Carmelita.

The villagers fell silent; even babies were hushed. Except for the priest who came to the village every month or two, visitors were rare.

Don Ignacio, attempting to recover his dignity, spoke boldly. "Every year it becomes harder to make a living from this poor land. The deer and quail that provide us with meat are harder to find. We must rid our valley and mountain of the flesh-eating animals that compete with us for food. The wolves, bears, and mountain lions cannot be allowed to take the food from our children's mouths."

The stranger looked about him at the dry fields and overgrazed land that surrounded the village. His gaze wandered to the mountain where the villagers had burned and cleared steep forested slopes to plant more corn. "Are you sure that your problems will be solved by killing the wild brothers and sisters?" the stranger simply asked.

"Yes," said Don Ignacio.

"Is there anyone who will speak for the wild creatures?" the stranger asked.

Don Miguel opened his mouth to speak, but was silenced by a harsh look from Don Ignacio. Don Miguel had not been born in the village. Although he had lived there for many years, he was not considered one of them.

"As you are all of one mind, your appeal has been heard." Again, the stranger regarded the eroded land all around him. "You have already put your foot on the path that will make your wish come true."

Don Ignacio smiled broadly. Only Don Miguel and the stranger sadly shook their heads.

As the stranger turned to leave, he paused briefly and said, "Your people say, *'Nadie sabe lo que tiene hasta que lo pierde.'* (A person does not appreciate what he has until he loses it.) If you ever seek what you have lost, look. . ." but his words were garbled by the noisy chatter of the villagers.

"Did you hear his last words, María?" In confusion, María shook her head at a troubled Don Miguel. He pushed his way through the crowd. But when he reached the grove of cottonwood trees, the man was gone.

Time pays no heed to events big or small, happy or sad, in people's lives. And so it was in the village. As the days passed into weeks and the weeks into months and then years, the stranger's visit became a dim memory faded by the villagers' struggle to plant and to harvest and to plant again.

BUT MARIA DID NOT FORGET

the stranger. As the village grew poorer, Don Miguel spent more and more time in the mountains. As the years passed, Don Miguel's hair and beard turned silvery white. He often asked María, "The stranger said 'look to the mountain.' Didn't he say that, María?"

María was sad for her friend, and her family. The village grew in numbers. With each passing year there was less fertile land on which to raise food. The villagers continued to cut and burn the forests to clear more land to plant corn. But the corn could not hold the soil. With spring rains the rich soil ran down the mountain sides to the valley floor. For a while the valley was rich, but soon only gravel and poor soil ran from the mountain and covered the valley. The corn shriveled in the sterile blanket of dirt. Clear streams that once flowed from the mountain dried up. And when the rains came, there were terrible floods.

As the stranger had predicted, the mountain lions, bears, and wolves were gone. And the deer and rabbits? With little food, water, and cover, they scrambled for each morsel of green. They ate the shrubs and, as high as they could reach, stripped the leaves and bark from the trees. Tiny seedlings struggling to break through the dry soil were nipped back to the root. And with no predators to take the weak and the sick animals, they suffered.

At night María's father would stand by the open door and say, "I cannot sleep. It is too still, too quiet. The howl of the wolf is gone, the scream of the mountain lion, the call of the owl. I cannot even imagine that I hear the bear snuffling for roots or drinking from the stream, because the bear is no longer there." He drew his wife close. "I feel the emptiness, too," she said. "*El encanto* (the enchantment) is gone."

One spring, María's youngest brother became very ill. The *curandera* touched his flushed cheeks and only shook her head. "I can no longer find the plant that cools a fever. I'm sorry, there is little that I can do."

"But this plant must still grow somewhere," said María.

The *curandera* shrugged her shoulders. "Perhaps high on the mountain, but I am too old to go there now."

"Describe it to me," said María.

The next morning María was awakened by the harsh sound of her brother's cough. Looking pale and worn herself, María's mother sat by his pallet. Searching for forage for their sheep, María's father and older brothers were gone. María quickly made tea and tortillas for her mother and brother and packed a small sack of food for herself.

"I will take papa's horse to the field," said María.

"You are a good girl, María. Be careful," her mother said wearily.

Riding bareback, María passed Don Miguel's tidy, white house. Although the old man was standing in the doorway, she did not look at him. He would ask where she was going, and she didn't want to lie to her friend.

But Don Miguel knew where María was going. The *curandera* had told the old man how scarce the healing plants were. She had nothing to help María's brother.

Shading his eyes from the sun's glare, Don Miguel studied the cloud of dust kicked up by María's horse. Finally, he turned to his old sorrel horse, Amigo, and his dog, Pedro. "Come on, you two. We cannot let María go alone to the mountain." Amigo nuzzled him affectionately, and the excited Pedro rolled in the dirt.

The day was long and hot for María. The girl was unaccustomed to riding long distances. By noon, when she dismounted, her legs felt sore and rubbery. By evening, she led the horse.

In the orange glow of a beautiful sunset, María tethered her horse and built a blazing fire. As María sat before the fire, she pulled her shawl more tightly about her shoulders. She had never been away from home overnight. With her large, loving family, she had seldom even been by herself. Now she was cold, alone, and afraid.

Suddenly, María heard a twig snap in the brush. Her heart began to pound. Looking past the fire's brightness, she squinted into the darkness. She pulled the shawl over her head. Perhaps if she could not see what was in the brush, it could not see her. The night was very quiet. María's curiosity was greater than her fear. She peeked through a tiny tear in her shawl. Standing on the other side of the fire was a man!

María could hear the pounding of her heart in her ears. The man was between her and her horse — she could not make a run for it. Then she must stand her ground. Trembling, she lowered the shawl from her head. The man moved into the firelight. María gasped. Though several years had passed since he had visited the village, the stranger in the rough, worn robes remained unchanged. The flames of the fire were reflected in his dark, ageless eyes. For a moment María's fear made her look away.

But like a swiftly rising tide, anger surged through María. "You did not help the villagers as you promised. Instead, you brought more hunger and sickness to their bodies, and more loneliness to their hearts."

The stranger spoke softly. "María, it is what the villagers wanted. Their hearts were closed to the enchantment that wild animals and wild places bring to our lives. With their words and actions, the villagers chose their path."

María's brown eyes snapped. "It was not the choice of *all* the villagers. You did not ask the children to choose."

The stranger looked startled. "What would the children choose, María? What would *you* choose?"

María's eyes glistened. "To bring back *el encanto.*"

The stranger smiled gently. "Only you can bring the enchantment back, María. Look into the fire."

As the stranger talked, pictures like those we have in dreams at night appeared in the flames.

The stranger said, "Mountain lions, bears, and wolves need water to drink and forests in which to make their homes. Your people must return the mountain to the wild creatures. Allow the forest to grow again. When the forest returns, it will feed the soil, and the soil will hold the water. Once again the water will flow gently to the valley below, and quench the thirst of the villagers and their crops. The needs of people, mountain lions, bears, and wolves are much the same."

Suddenly, Don Miguel stepped into the circle of light. "I searched for you for years. Why didn't you come to me?" The old man spoke with a feeling of betrayal and defeat.

"I'm sorry, Don Miguel, but your courage failed you. You allowed others to make your choices for you. Do not look to the mountain, Don Miguel, look to yourself." The stranger smiled gently. "María will need your wisdom and experience. Help her and the others bring back *el encanto*."

María ran to Don Miguel and threw her arms around him. When she looked back at the fire, the stranger was gone.

The next morning, Don Miguel and María ate a quick breakfast of cold tortillas. They did not speak of the stranger. From the many years spent on the mountain, the old man knew of a steep and protected area where the deer and rabbits might not have nibbled away the plant María needed for her brother.

The morning was chilly. Pedro ran ahead of them. Suddenly the dog began to bark excitedly. "What is that fool into now?" Don Miguel asked. María and the old man urged their horses forward.

The old man helped María down from her horse, and they carefully made their way through a thorny thicket. Finally they found Pedro barking at the base of a steep rock wall. The old man looked up.

He shaded his eyes from the sun's glare. Suddenly he laughed and said, "María, look! Look up on the ledge!"

María squinted hard in the bright sunlight. And then she laughed with delight. Standing on the rock ledge, nervously twitching its tail from side to side, was a mountain lion.

The lion's tawny coat glistened in the sun. As the lion paced on the ledge, its muscles rippled evenly and powerfully under its smooth, short fur. Its head seemed small compared to the long, lean body. Its tail, looking as if the end had been dipped in black paint, was very long. Its amber eyes were keen and anxious. Occasionally the cat lifted its upper lip and, showing large white teeth, snarled at the barking dog.

María turned to Don Miguel. "*El encanto* — it's returning to the mountain."

The old man smiled broadly. For a moment, the excitement of discovery and wonder allowed him to touch that place of childhood we hold deep within our grown-up selves.

DON MIGUEL AND I

returned to the village from the high place on the mountain where we found the plant to cure my brother. Today I live far from my village, the mountains, and the rushing stream. Once I asked my aging mother about the stranger and the bad years in our village. She would not talk about them. She said maybe I dreamed this story.

As I look around me now, I know that my story is true. The message of the stranger is clear to me. We are a wonderful people. We send men and women where only the stars once lived. We heal the sick with powerful medicines. We create machines with minds similar to ours. We steal secrets from the sun. But in all that is new, we must not forget what is old. The lion, the stream, the mountain, and the sky are a part of us, and we a part of them. What we do to them, we do to ourselves.

THE END

The proverbs quoted in "El Encanto" were taken from Mexican Proverbs *by Octavio A. Ballesteros, 1979, Eakin Press, Austin, Texas.*

Activities with the *lions*

YOU WILL FIND "FACT tracks" on the following pages. They will give you interesting bits of information about mountain lions. These facts will help you solve the maze at the end of this book.

The mountain lion is digitigrade. It stands and runs on its toes.

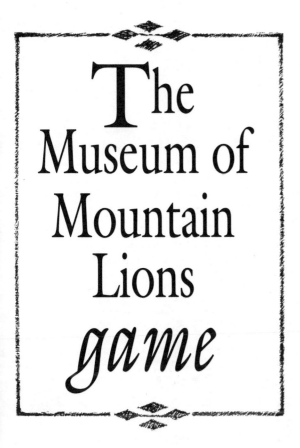

The Museum of Mountain Lions *game*

Purpose

Museums are fun and exciting places to learn about our planet and the plants, animals, and people that share it. If mountain lions and other large predators are to survive, our first responsibility is to learn as much as we can about these amazing animals. Visiting a museum is a good place to start. Armed with knowledge, we can discard the myths created about predators and can make better management decisions. As future scientists, voters, politicians, and wildlife managers, we must cooperate and always be conscious of time. For as time passes and decisions are *not* made, more wildlife habitat is lost.

The Museum of Mountain Lions Game includes:

- The Game Board (pages 16 and 17)
- The Clue Sheet (pages 19 and 20)
- The Answer Wheel (page 21)
- Mountain Lion Puzzle, Numbered Squares, and Tokens (pages 22 and 23)

Before Playing

1. Cut out both pages of the playing board along the dashed line.
2. Tape the pages together so they will lie flat.
3. Remove the Clue Sheet from the book by cutting along the dashed line.
4. Cut out and assemble the Answer Wheel on page 21.
5. Color the mountain lion and cut out the puzzle pieces on page 23. Place on the board in three piles.
6. Cut out the numbered squares. Put them in a paper sack.
7. Cut out and assemble tokens.

When you have finished playing, keep all game pieces and the board together in a 9" x 12" envelope so you can play again.

The Museum of Mountain Lions *game*

Rules

1. Place token on ENTER. Draw a number and advance in either direction.

2. When you land on a paw print, choose a symbol from within the room. Read the statement from the Clue Sheet that has a matching symbol. Decide if it is true or false.

Objective

For 1-4 players

As players move through the rooms of the museum, the object of the game is to collect all puzzle pieces in order to build the mountain lion. Players must always be conscious of time. Within the 20-minute time limit, they must collect all puzzle pieces, race to the finish line, and then assemble the mountain lion.

To be successful, players must cooperate. Respecting each other's opinions, they discuss whether statements are true or false. As a group, they piece together the mountain lion. Players win or lose as a team. Similarly, if we succeed in saving the earth's predators, we all will be winners!

If you choose to be solitary like the mountain lion, you may play this game alone. You are competing not with other players, but against time.

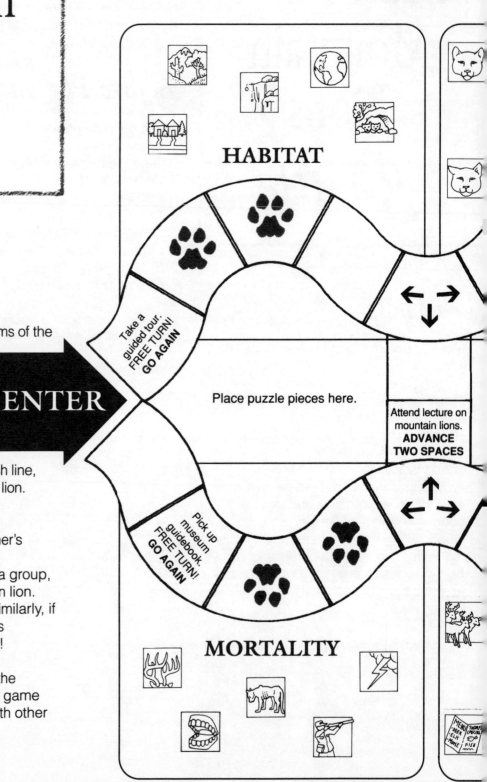

HABITAT

Take a guided tour. FREE TURN! **GO AGAIN**

ENTER

Place puzzle pieces here.

Attend lecture on mountain lions. **ADVANCE TWO SPACES**

Pick up museum guidebook. FREE TURN! **GO AGAIN**

MORTALITY

16

3. Dial the Answer Wheel to the category of the room. Then find the matching symbol. If you answer correctly, take a puzzle piece.

4. When you land on a space with arrows, you may go forward, backward, or across.

5. When all puzzle pieces have been collected, take turns drawing numbers and move quickly to the EXIT.

6. When all players have exited, put the puzzle together. You and your teammates win if the puzzle is completed before your time is up!

COMMUNICATION

Share with friends what you've learned. **ADVANCE ONE SPACE**

HUNTING

Ask guard for directions. **ADVANCE TWO SPACES**

Place puzzle pieces here.

Place puzzle pieces here.

Stop to have lunch at cafeteria. **LOSE NEXT TURN**

Buy souvenir in museum shop. **LOSE NEXT TURN**

EXIT

Now build your Mountain Lion!

Read all the exhibit labels. **ADVANCE ONE SPACE**

FOOD

MATING & THE YOUNG

YOU MAY PLAY THE
game over and over again. As you learn more about mountain lions and how to cooperate with your teammates, it will be easier to make it to the finish line and complete the puzzle within the allotted time. Try to finish in less time. To determine your best time, keep a record in this table.

Mountain lions live from sea level to elevations of over 11,000 feet (3350 meters).

Museum of Mountain Lions
RECORD OF VISITS

Date:

Visitors (players):

Start: Finish: TOTAL TIME:

Date:

Visitors (players):

Start: Finish: TOTAL TIME:

Date:

Visitors (players):

Start: Finish: TOTAL TIME:

Date:

Visitors (players):

Start: Finish: TOTAL TIME:

Clue Sheet (True or False Statements – You Decide!)

MORTALITY

 Weak kittens in a litter, independent young cats hunting for themselves for the first time, old animals, and mountain lions without an established territory often die of starvation.

 The weapons of prey animals such as hooves and antlers present no threat to mountain lions. When attacking prey, mountain lions are never injured or killed.

 Being hunted is one of the main causes of death to mountain lions. People driving automobiles also contribute to mountain lion mortality.

 Mountain lions can die from accidents — drowning, lightning, collision with tree branches while running, and poisonous snakes.

 In the wild, mountain lions never suffer from the problems of old age such as arthritis or worn teeth.

HABITAT

 The mountain lion is very adaptable. It lives in a variety of habitats: swamps, deserts, mountains, open woodlands, and jungles.

 In keeping with their secretive nature, mountain lions prefer areas of heavy cover, or rugged country with rocky cliffs and ledges.

 When mountain lion habitat is taken over by humans, these cats simply crowd more closely together and share their territories.

 In the wild, mountain lions can be found all over the world.

 The mother raises the young alone. She prepares a simple den under a fallen log, in dense vegetation, or under a rock ledge in the mountains.

FOOD

 Depending upon where they live, their age, experience, and hunting ability, mountain lions prey on a number of different animals.

 Mountain lions feed on deer (mule and white-tailed), elk, porcupines, bighorn sheep, pronghorns, moose, squirrels, beaver, marmots, mice, snowshoe hares, armadillos, skunks, and fish.

 How often a mountain lion must kill to eat varies. Lions prefer fresh meat. They may kill more often during summer when heat causes meat to spoil quickly.

 Lion kills over a year range from one deer a week to one deer every three to four weeks. The lion supplements its deer diet with smaller animals.

 In the few areas where they occur together, grizzly and black bears, wolverines, bobcats, and coyotes do not compete with mountain lions for food.

 Grizzly and black bears, wolverines, bobcats, coyotes, as well as scavengers such as eagles, weasels, and ravens do not benefit from the left-overs of a lion's kill.

 Vegetation such as grass and berries is never part of a mountain lion's diet.

COMMUNICATION

 When the mountain lion's ears are "up," the animal is communicating pleasure.

 When the lion's ears are pressed flat against its head, the lion is signaling its intent to attack.

 When the ears are halfway in between and the pupils of the eyes contract to slits, the lion is in a threatening posture.

19

When the ears move about with changing facial expressions, the animal is confused.

 Lions vocalize with chirps, peeps, whistles, growls, screams, and purrs.

 To make other mountain lions aware of their territorial claims, these cats vocalize and communicate with scent. They leave behind their "sign" — scrapes or scratches, dung heaps, and claw marks on trees.

 Although conflicts between lions sometimes arise, communication allows these powerful animals to remain aware of each other and to avoid one another.

HUNTING

 Like wolves, mountain lions hunt in packs.

 When hunting, lions often move in a zigzag fashion over their range. The cat usually approaches prey by stalking. Taking advantage of available cover, the lion moves closer to its prey until it is within striking distance.

 When attacking deer, the cat extends its claws and grasps the shoulders and neck of its victim with its front feet. The hind feet are either on the animal's flanks or on the ground for stability. The lion kills its prey by biting the back of the neck, which usually breaks the neck.

 Mountain lions hunt only at night — never in daylight.

 Lions are generally more active at night. They usually bed down in midday in thick brush or under rocky ledges.

 In many areas of the West, mountain lions follow the seasonal migration of their main prey, mule deer. Mountain lions move with the mule deer from high elevations in summer to lower elevations in winter.

 Mountain lions have an unfair advantage because prey species are unable to defend themselves.

MATING & THE YOUNG

 In the northern Rockies, mountain lion kittens are born during the late spring, summer, or early fall. But, throughout their range, mountain lions may have litters any time of the year.

 Litters vary in size from one to six kittens, but usually average three kittens.

 The kittens' eyes remain closed for about two weeks after birth.

 Kittens thrive entirely on their mother's milk for almost six weeks.

 At about six to eight weeks of age, the mother first leads the young to a carcass. They usually remain on the kill until it is eaten, and then move on. They do not return to the den.

 The mother teaches the young to hunt. Because it must depend on its mother for food and protection, an orphaned kitten will probably not survive unless it is at least six months old.

 Young mountain lions generally separate from the mother when they are one to two years old.

 Mountain lions are normally solitary animals. However, male and female mountain lions accept each other for brief periods in order to mate.

Museum of Mountain Lions Answer Wheel

CUT OUT BOTH CIRCLES ALONG

the dashed lines, being sure to cut the notch in the smaller circle. Place the smaller circle with the notch in it over the big circle with the pictures. Line up the X's in the center. Poke a brad through the X's with the head of the brad on top. Fold the ends of the brad open underneath. Now you can dial the wheel to find if your answers to the clues are correct!

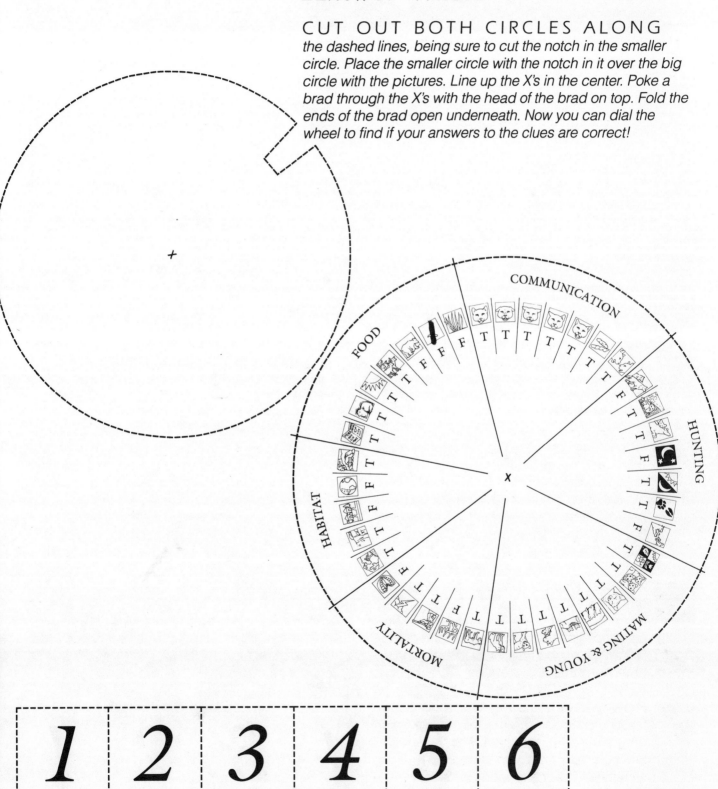

1 2 3 4 5 6

| 6 | 5 | 4 | 3 | 2 | 1 |

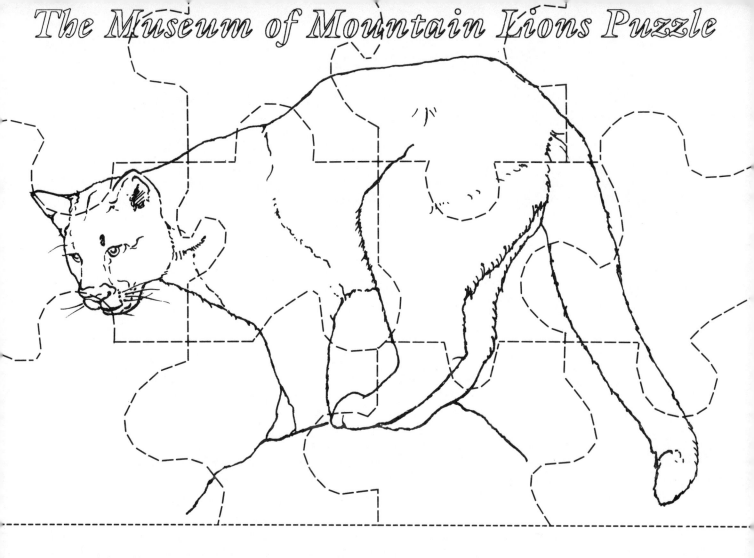

The Museum of Mountain Lions Tokens

COLOR THE

characters. Cut out the characters and stands along the dashed lines. Don't forget to cut the dashed slots. Fold characters in half, lining up slots and placing on stands. You can now play the role of scientist, voter, politician, or wildlife manager as you go through the Museum of Mountain Lions collecting the information you need to piece together the puzzle of the mountain lion.

Characters

Stands

The Cat of Many *names*

PANTHER, PAINTER, *mountain lion, cougar, puma, catamount . . .*

The English language has over 40 different names for mountain lions. Spanish and Indian dialects have about 60. The common name depends upon place and time in history.

Mountain lion kittens are born with their eyes closed. They are fully furred with spotted coats and short, ringed tails.

IN 1502, COLUMBUS IDENTIFIED this tan, maneless cat as "lion" because it resembled the African lioness. During colonial times in the area that later became New York State, the animal was called "tiger." Mountain men and fur trappers of the early 1800s called it "painter" (probably a distortion of the name "panther").

In Mexico the cat is called *león, leopardo,* or *puma.* In the Rocky Mountain West, "mountain lion" is the preferred name, and in the Pacific Northwest, "cougar." East of the Mississippi the cat is known as "catamount" or "panther." "Catamount," a New England term, is the abbreviated form for "cat of the mountain."

The English translation of many Indian terms shows the early Native Americans' respect for the cat as a hunter: "greatest of wild hunters," "lord of the forest," "the cat of god," "father of game."

Imagine that you have not cleaned your room for a year. One day you come home from school and find all your possessions in a pile in the middle of the floor. Your mother indicates a number of empty boxes and, closing the door behind her, says, "I want this room neat and *orderly.*" Standing beside this huge pile of "stuff," you scratch your head and ask, "How do I do this?"

Simple! You classify. You organize your "stuff" into groups. First you decide what the categories will be: ACTION FIGURES, ELECTRONIC GAMES, PUPPETS, ART SUPPLIES. Then you remove the first item from the pile and, depending upon its characteristics, decide to which group it belongs. The first item is a watercolor brush. It has none of the characteristics of an action figure, an electronic game, or a puppet — it belongs in ART SUPPLIES.

Scientists have done the same thing with the plants and animals of our earth. Zoologists use the size, color, skull measurements, and many other characteristics of animals to organize them into groups and to arrive at their scientific names. Even though animals and plants often have several common names, they have only one scientific name. Using the method of scientific classification, let's see how scientists arrived at the name *Felis concolor* for the mountain lion.

THINK OF THE

classification system as a funnel. It is very wide at the top and narrows to a small opening at the bottom. If you pour all the animals into the funnel and classify them properly, only *Felis concolor* will drop out at the bottom. Let's look at a few of the obvious characteristics of each level.

This creature belongs to the kingdom **Animalia** (an-uh-MAYL-yuh). It is not a plant, a one-celled organism, or a fungus (mushrooms, molds, yeast). It is an animal.

This animal has a backbone, so it is in the phylum **Chordata** (KOHRD-uht-uh). (The animal kingdom has more than 20 phyla.)

This animal belongs to the class **Mammalia** (muh-MAYL-yuh), because it has hair and nourishes its young with milk.

This animal eats flesh, so it is in the order **Carnivora** (kahr-NIHV-uh-ruh).

This animal is in the cat family **Felidae** (FEE-luhd-uh) because it has a short snout and short-haired tail. Also, it has five toes on the front feet and four on the back feet, claws that are retractable, large canine teeth, few cheek teeth (premolars and molars located in the cheek area of the mouth), and large eyes with vertically contracting pupils.

The genus of this animal is **Felis** (FEE-luhs). Cats in the genus *Felis* are small to large carnivores (KAHR-nuh-vohrz) (meat-eaters) that are digitigrade (DIHJ-uht-uh-grayd) (walk on digits, or toes), have large feet, large eyes, and well-developed ears. The coat is tawny or patterned with spots or stripes.

The species is **concolor** (KAHN-kuhl-uhr). *Felis concolor* (the mountain lion) is the largest species in the genus *Felis*. Its coat is yellowish-brown (tawny) above and white on the underside.

KINGDOM

PHYLUM

CLASS

ORDER

FAMILY

GENUS

SPECIES

Try to find Felis concolor *on your own.*

LOOK AT THE PUZZLE.

Start with "kingdom." Color every space in the puzzle with the mountain lion's kingdom (Animalia) brown or tan. Do the same for each level of classification (phylum, class, order, family, genus, and species).

The mountain lion is very secretive. But by classifying it correctly, you can find it in this puzzle.

At birth, kittens weigh about one pound (0.45 kilograms).

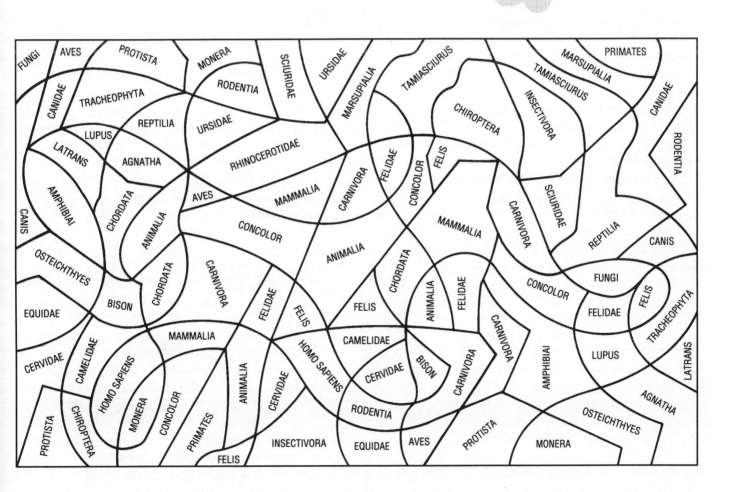

Lineage of *lions*

HAVE YOU EVER HEARD the expression, *"to fight like cats and dogs"? Cartoon characters such as Garfield and Odie and Heathcliff and Spike make us laugh at the natural hostility that seems to exist between dogs and cats. However, dogs and cats have much in common. They both are meat eaters and belong to the order Carnivora. They also share a common ancestor. Scientists believe that a group of small, tree-dwelling creatures from the family Miacidae gave rise to the carnivores. Miacids probably lived about 50 million years ago!*

MEMBERS OF THE CAT FAMILY emerged about 40 million years ago. The family split into two lines — "modern cats" and the now extinct saber-toothed cats.

Modern cats are divided into three groups:
1. BIG CATS (*Panthera*) include the lion, tiger, leopard, and jaguar.
2. SMALL CATS (*Felis*) include the cougar, lynx, bobcat, ocelot, and our pet cats.
3. CHEETAHS (*Acinonyx*) are in a group by themselves.

One characteristic that distinguishes these groups is that big cats can roar, but purr only when they exhale, or breathe out. Small cats can purr, but cannot roar. Although the cheetah is often grouped with the big cats, it cannot roar, but purrs very loudly!

Big cats

LION (*Panthera leo*) — Lions live in groups called prides. They prefer the open spaces of Africa such as savannas and desert fringes. Lions do not live in tropical jungles. A small  group of Asiatic lions (an endangered species) inhabits India's Gir Forest sanctuary. Females are the better hunters, and males and females defend the pride's territory. Only the male lion has a mane.

Base Coat Color: brownish-yellow (like dry grass)
Special Markings: black behind the ears, black tuft at the end of the tail

TIGER (*Panthera tigris*) — The tiger is the largest cat in the world. The Siberian tiger can weigh over 600 pounds (272 kilograms) and exceed 12 feet (3.7 meters) in length. A single tiger can eat 90 pounds (41 kilograms) of meat in one  day! Tigers live in the forested regions of Asia. Because of conflicts with humans and habitat destruction, the tiger's numbers have been greatly reduced. A few subspecies face extinction.

Base Coat Color: brownish-yellow to orange-red
Special Markings: black stripes; white fur on throat, underbody, and insides of legs

A UNIQUE CAT IN A group by itself is the **CHEETAH** *(Acinonyx jubatus)*. The gentle cheetah suffers from other predators that steal its food and kill its young. The life expectancy of a cheetah in the wild is only four to five years. Speed is its primary defense. Fastest of the cats, it exceeds speeds of 60 miles (97 kilometers) per hour. "Tear lines," dark lines that run from the cheetah's eyes to the corners of its mouth, probably shield the eyes from the sun's glare. With farms taking over the grasslands and poachers

hunting it for its skin, cheetahs may not exist in the wild by the twenty-first century.

Base Coat Color: brownish-yellow, except the throat and underparts are white
Special Markings: The coat is dotted with solid black spots.

The mountain lion's tail is important for balance. It is more than one-third the lion's total length, from the nose to the tip of the tail.

LEOPARD *(Panthera pardus)*—Of the big cats, the leopard is the most elusive and adaptable. Its habitat ranges from frigid mountain peaks to humid jungles to deserts. The leopard avoids open spaces. Its black, spotted yellow, or white coat blends with brushy or forested backgrounds. One

leopard, the snow leopard, lives in a very specialized habitat — the bleak alpine areas of central Asia. The snow leopard faces an uncertain future. It is hunted for its beautiful coat to satisfy the fashion market.

Base Coat Color: yellow, white, or light tan
Special Markings: black spots grouped in small circles, called rosettes

JAGUAR *(Panthera onca)* — In remote areas, jaguars range from northern Mexico to nearly the southern tip of South America. Once a cat of the southwestern United States, human activities have eliminated the jaguar north of the border. Skilled

hunters, jaguars have been known to take a 100-pound (45-kilogram) capybara, the largest rodent on earth; peccary, a piglike animal with powerful tusks; and even the caiman, a reptile similar to the alligator.

Base Coat Color: brownish-yellow or golden
Special Markings: Rosettes along the back and sides are light in color and have one or more extra spots within the rosette. Spots are completely black on the head, legs, and underside.

Small cats

MOUNTAIN LION *(Felis concolor)* — The secretive nature of this animal is expressed in its folk names — "ghost of the wilderness," or "ghost walker." The mountain lion feeds on deer, elk, mountain sheep, beavers, and porcupines. Although originally among the most widely distributed North

American land mammals, its range has been greatly reduced. The Florida panther, with only about 30 individuals alive today, is probably one of the most endangered mammals on earth.

Base Coat Color: tawny above, white underside
Special Markings: black on tip of tail and behind ears, white upper lip

A FAMILIAR SMALL CAT is the **DOMESTIC CAT** (*Felis domesticus*) — The early Egyptians tamed the African wildcat, from which our pet cats are descended. Cats were considered sacred in Egypt. The penalty for killing a cat was death! During the Middle Ages, cats were associated with evil and witchcraft. People had many superstitions about cats. Eventually people realized the important role that cats played in reducing the number of rats and mice. Cats are

certainly appreciated today — over 40 million cats are pets in the United States alone!

Base Coat Color: varies—white, black, gray, silver, reddish-brown
Special Markings: spots, blotches, stripes

BOBCAT (*Felis rufus*) — In North America the bobcat can be found in a variety of habitats — forests, deserts, and swamps

(such as the Florida Everglades). Bobcats are known to live close to dense human populations. Like other members of the cat family that move about mostly at night, the bobcat is seldom seen by people.

Base Coat Color: tan to reddish-brown with black streaks or spots
Special Markings: white underside with black spots, white underside of tail

LYNX (*Felis lynx*) — With its snowshoe-like foot (large and

padded with hair), the lynx is well adapted to its life of cold and snow. The North American lynx almost exclusively hunts snowshoe hares for food. The lynx also lives in Asia and Europe.

Base Coat Color: Upper body parts grayish-brown blended with light brown, top of head brown
Special Markings: The outside of the ears is brown with black edges and black tufts. The inside of the ears has a central white spot. The throat and ruff around the face are grayish-white, brown, and black. The paws, legs, and underparts of the cat are gray or buffy white. The insides of the legs are sometimes speckled with brown spots. The tip of the tail is black.

OCELOT (*Felis pardalis*) — This cat has been called the "painted leopard" because of the black rosettes and stripes that decorate its coat. It has been a victim of the fashion industry because of its beautiful pelt. Ocelots have been

observed hunting in pairs. They even appear to share the responsibilities of raising the young. Ocelots are found from the Texas border to the rain forests of South America.

Base Coat Color: reddish-yellow to grayish-white
Special Markings: black spots on the legs and paws, oval-shaped markings of reddish-yellow or grayish-white on other parts of the body, pink nose

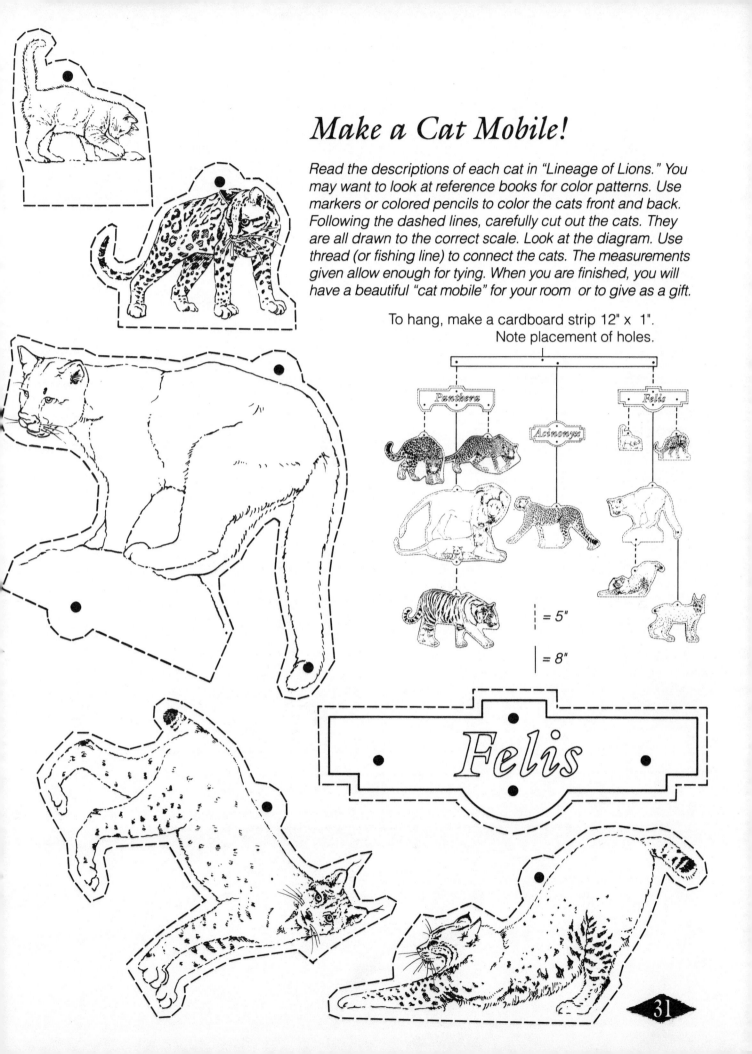

Make a Cat Mobile!

Read the descriptions of each cat in "Lineage of Lions." You may want to look at reference books for color patterns. Use markers or colored pencils to color the cats front and back. Following the dashed lines, carefully cut out the cats. They are all drawn to the correct scale. Look at the diagram. Use thread (or fishing line) to connect the cats. The measurements given allow enough for tying. When you are finished, you will have a beautiful "cat mobile" for your room or to give as a gift.

To hang, make a cardboard strip 12" x 1".
Note placement of holes.

Panthera

Acinonyx

Felis

= 5"

= 8"

Felis

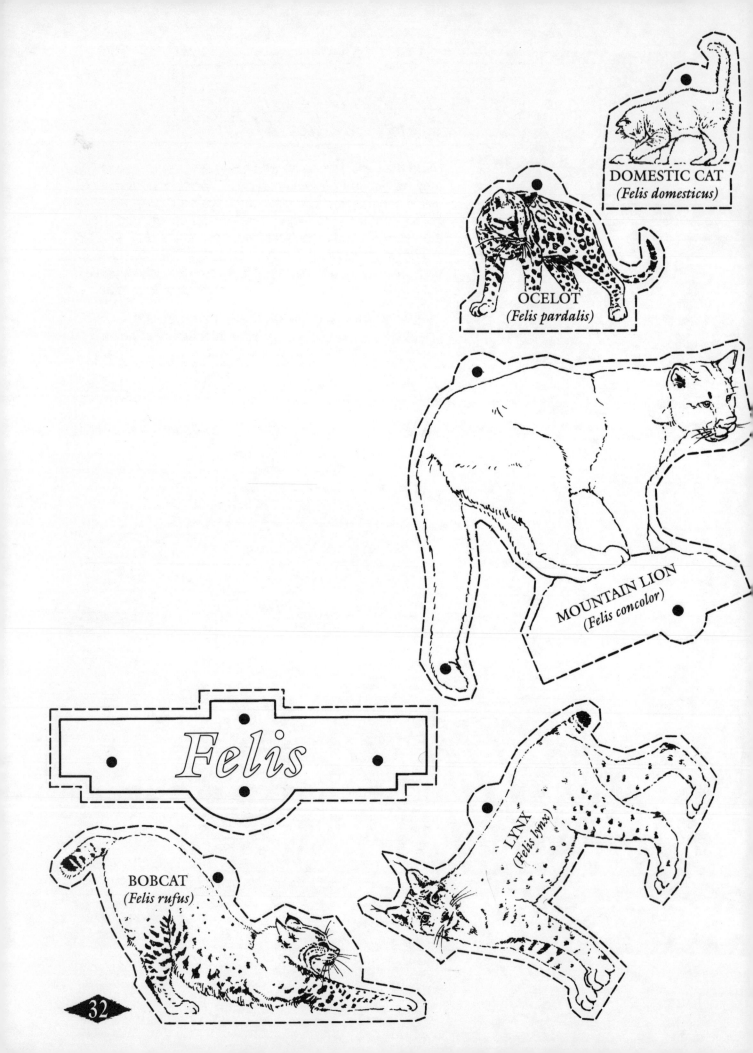

DOMESTIC CAT
(Felis domesticus)

OCELOT
(Felis pardalis)

MOUNTAIN LION
(Felis concolor)

Felis

LYNX
(Felis lynx)

BOBCAT
(Felis rufus)

32

Panthera

33

Panthera

JAGUAR
(Panthera

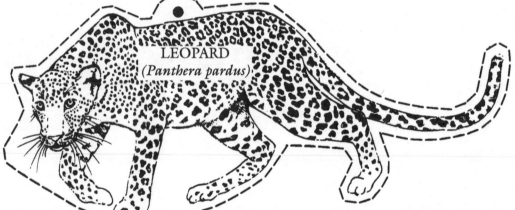

LEOPARD
(Panthera pardus)

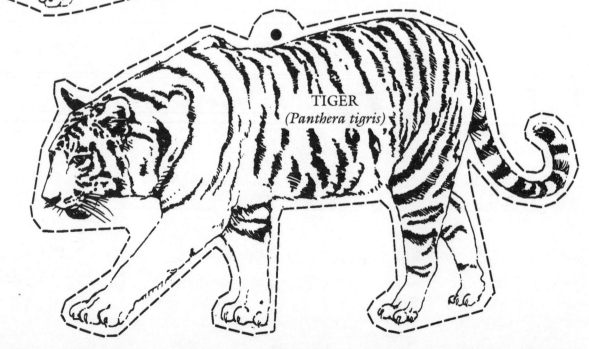

TIGER
(Panthera tigris)

Acinonyx

35

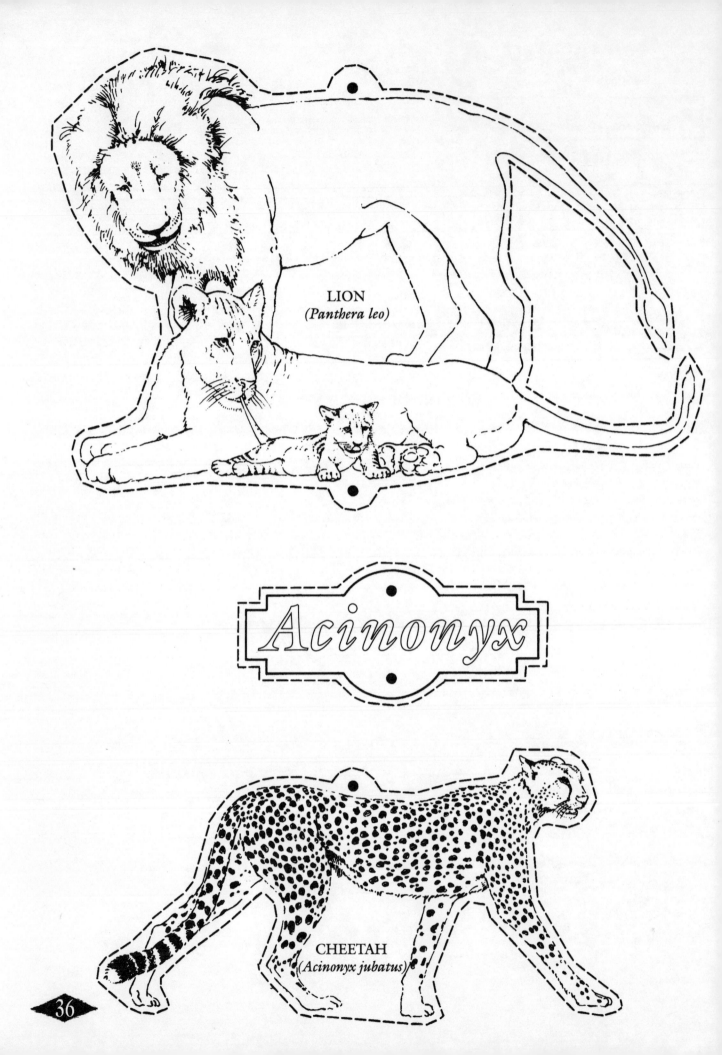

LION
(*Panthera leo*)

Acinonyx

CHEETAH
(*Acinonyx jubatus*)

The Lion That Couldn't *roar*

WHAT DOES A HUNTER NEED TO be successful? The hunter needs strength, speed, stealth, and the proper weapons. The mountain lion cannot roar like the tiger and African lion. However, its inability to roar does not diminish its hunting ability one bit. The mountain lion's body is strong—lean and well muscled with sturdy limbs.

Mountain lions are sprinters, not long-distance runners. The speed that they exhibit when sprinting is partly the result of their long stride. Three features combine to create this stride: (see the picture below) (1) The mountain lion's legs are long. (2) Lions walk on their toes, or digits, so the rest of the foot adds to the length of their leg. Longer legs make for a longer stride. (Your dog and cat are "digitigrade," [DIHJ-uht-uh-grayd] but you are "plantigrade" [PLANT-uh-grayd]. You stand on the soles of your feet. Walk on your toes; see how much longer your legs appear.) (3) The animal has a very flexible spine. As the mountain lion brings its back feet forward, the backbone bends (flexes) to such a degree that the hind feet can be placed ahead of the front feet. This feature also contributes to the lion's ability to leap great distances.

Surprise is an important element for the hunter that stalks its prey. The lion's paw is designed for stealth. The spongy toe, central pads, and hair that covers the bottom of the paw (except for the pads) allow the lion to walk quietly. The claws are "retractable" (rih-TRAK-tuh-buhl). Muscles attached to the cat's claws withdraw them into pockets in the animal's foot. Lions extend their claws only when needed. This practice serves two purposes: the claws remain sharp, and the animal pads noiselessly even on hard surfaces.

THE MOUNTAIN LION

was revered for its skill as a hunter among many early tribes of Native Americans. On the eve of a boy's first hunt, he might receive from his grandfather a bracelet made from the dewclaw of the mountain lion. Then the boy — like the lion — would be a great hunter. Indians made quivers (cases for arrows) from the skins of many animals including deer, wolf, and coyote. A quiver made from the hide of a mountain lion was the most highly prized.

3

1

2

WHAT ARE THE MOUNTAIN LION'S

weapons? The dewclaw, a digit that is found above the foot on the inside of the front leg, is curved and very sharp.

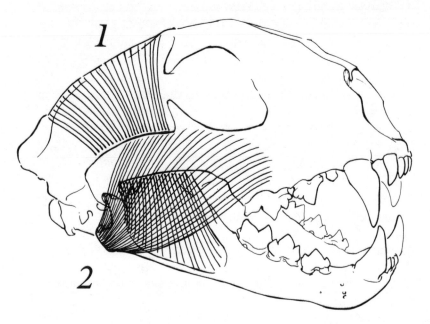

A study of the mountain lion's skull reveals more "weapons." This cat has 30 teeth. The over-sized canines generally inflict the bite to the back of the neck, which kills large prey. The cat's molars slice the meat into pieces that are swallowed whole. The jaw is moved by strong muscles in the head. Note where the muscles are attached on the skull and jaw. The temporalis (tehm-puh-RAL-uhs) muscle (1) lifts the jaw up and back. The masseter (muh-SEET-uhr) muscle (2) lifts the jaw up and forward.

Locate the eye sockets on the skull. The lion's eyes are close together and face forward. This arrangement limits the lion's total field of view but gives the lion greater accuracy when attacking prey. In a sense, the mountain lion must "aim" its entire body in order to strike its prey. The eye placement allows the lion to better judge depth and distance. A deer's eyes, on the other hand, are located on the sides of its head. The deer is more aware of what is moving around it — such as a mountain lion!

Mountain lions are skillful at killing porcupines. They flip them over to expose their unprotected bellies.

The mountain lion's eyes are designed for day and night vision. The cat may hunt in sunshine or moonlight. The large pupil allows the eye to collect any available light. A special layer inside the eye, called the tapetum (tuh-PEET-uhm), acts like a mirror to bounce the light back through the visual cells. The large pupil and tapetum provide cats with good night vision. To protect the eye from too much light during the day, the animal's pupil contracts to a slit.

Internally, the mountain lion is also fit for the hunting life. Most predators live a "feast or famine" existence. The lion's stomach and esophagus can stretch to accommodate large meals. The cat quickly processes its food in its short digestive system. The lion's rough tongue allows it to lick any remaining meat from the bones of its kill.

However, inexperienced lions often suffer with porcupine quills in their paws or head. Some cats learn this skill better than others.

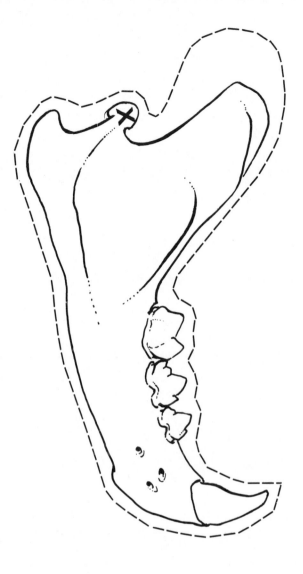

Make a mountain lion skull!

Cut out the mountain lion skull and jaw (mandible) along the dashed lines. On the skull, carefully cut along the dashed line above the solid curved line (the zygomatic arch).

Place the jaw behind the skull. Slip the upper portion of the jaw through the slot in the skull.

Line up the X's on the skull and jaw. Push a brad through the X's. Open the brad to hold the skull and jaw together.

CLOSED

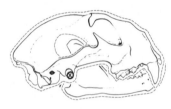

OPEN

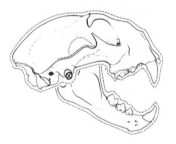

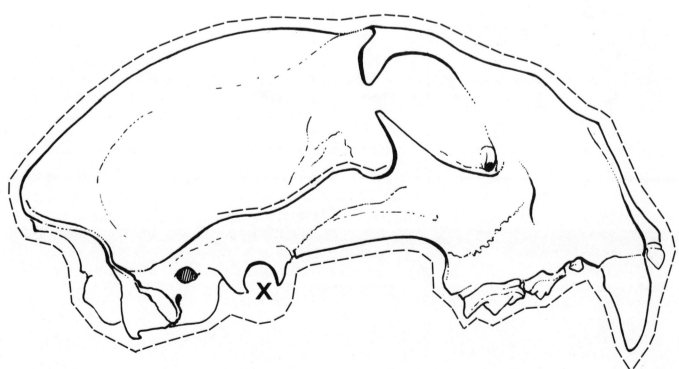

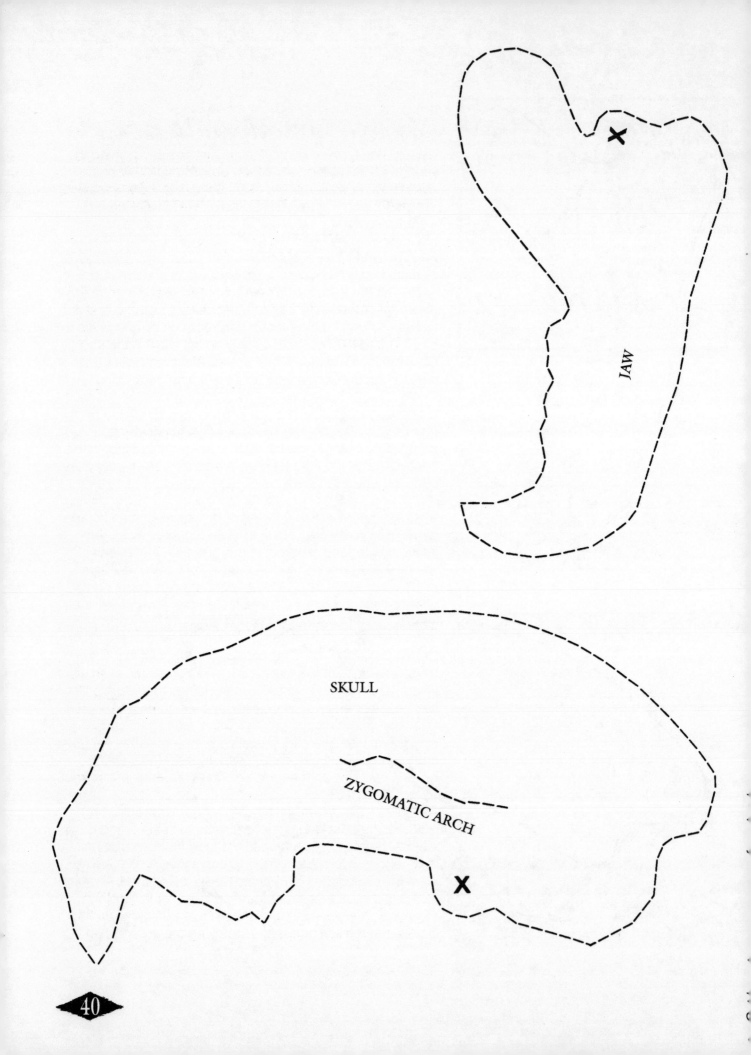

JAW

SKULL

ZYGOMATIC ARCH

40

Sign of the lion

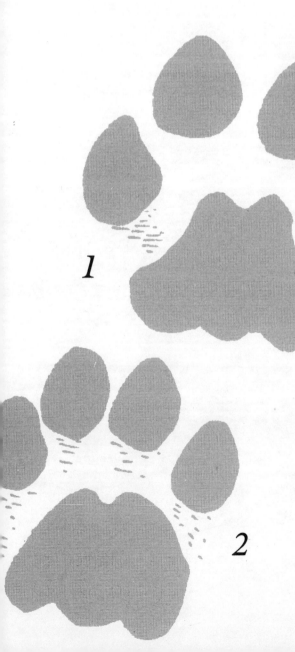

1

2

ZORRO,* THE MASKED MAN OF the Old West, rescued maidens in distress and righted the wrongs committed by a crooked governor in California's early days. Few people ever saw Zorro, but there was never any doubt about where he had been. He always left his signature behind — a large "Z" cut with his sword.

Like Zorro, the mountain lion is seldom seen and also leaves its mark behind. The lion's most obvious "signature" is its track. The track left by the front paw of a full-grown male lion measures about 3 -1/2 inches (8.9 centimeters) long and 4 inches (10 centimeters) wide. (The tracks on this page are full size.) The lion's front claws usually do not show in the track. Claw prints may occur if the lion slips and then extends its claws to recover its balance, or if the animal is climbing.

Compare the front and hind prints pictured. The front print (1) is slightly larger than the back (2). When walking, particularly in snow, the cat often places its hind foot in the print made by the front foot. Tail marks as well as tracks are often left behind in the snow.

After the mountain lion urinates or defecates, it may scrape dirt with its paws as a signal to other mountain lions. An interesting legend grew out of this practice. A Mexican worker told Stanley Young, author of the book *The Puma, Mysterious American Cat*, that the droppings of the puma changed into precious stones. The animal covered its scat so that these gems would not be found.

Depending upon where the lion lives and what it has eaten, the appearance of the scat varies. In dry areas (such as the southwestern United States), the droppings may be in pellet form. In other areas, it may be segmented cords with short tails. The droppings may contain bone, teeth, hair, and sometimes plant material. Mountain lions sometimes eat grass and berries. Some biologists have suggested that eating grass clears parasites from the mountain lion's digestive tract.

A mountain lion maintains a home range. This range includes the area where the lion rests, hunts, and finds mates. Instead of defending territories with open combat, lions tend to avoid each other. To prevent a "run-in" and to mark the boundaries of its home range, a lion uses *scrapes* as signals to other animals, particularly other lions of the same sex. A scrape (or *scratch*) is a pile of dirt, twigs, and leaves that the lion builds by scratching the ground with

*The masked hero Zorro was the original creation of Johnston McCulley for his story "The Curse of Capistrano," in 1919.

its hind or front feet. Sometimes the lion urinates or defecates on top of the pile.

After it kills, the lion often drags its prey under a tree or to some hidden spot. When it has eaten all that it can, the cat will cover the carcass with dirt, leaves, and twigs. The lion may be attempting to hide its food supply from scavengers or this activity may actually keep the meat fresher for the next feeding. In the area around a carcass, the cats may bury their droppings. The covered droppings are called dung heaps.

Mountain lions sometimes leave claw marks on trees. The reason they do this is unclear.

See how good a lion hunter you are!

Cameras only, please! Think of all the different ways the lion leaves its "signature" behind: tracks, scat, scrapes, covered carcasses, dung heaps, and claw marks on trees. Look at the picture. How many examples of the mountain lion's signature can you find? Tell a story about the picture. See the answer key on page 62.

The Animals' court

Make Animals' Court puppets!

Color the characters. Cut them out along the outside dashed lines. Carefully cut along the dashed lines inside the figures to create two slits. Place the puppets on your fingers as shown below. By placing a puppet on each finger, you may perform the puppet show on the following pages by yourself. Or, have your friends help you.

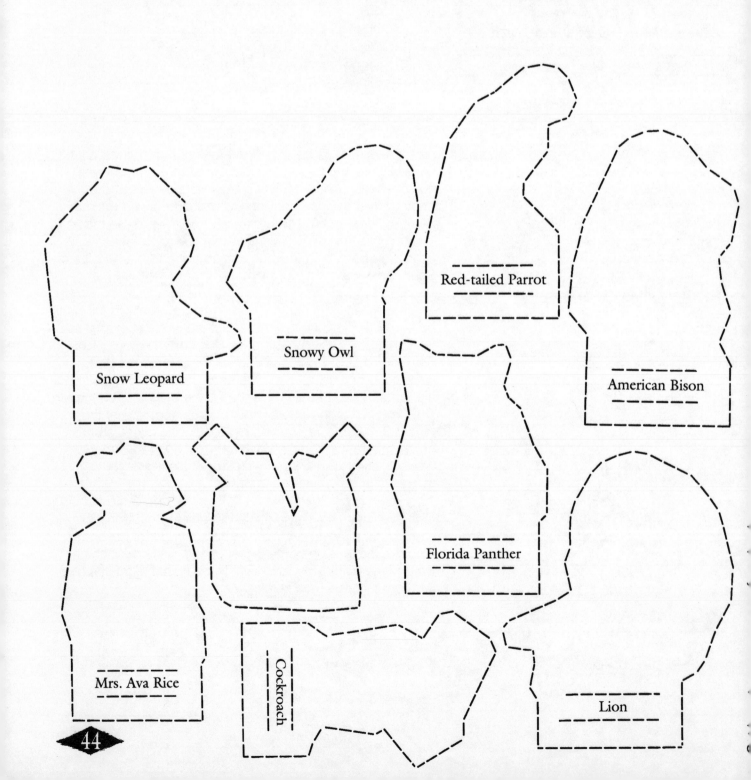

Red-tailed Parrot

Snowy Owl

Snow Leopard

American Bison

Florida Panther

Mrs. Ava Rice

Cockroach

Lion

IN THE STORY

"El Encanto," *the villagers exhausted the soil with poor farming practices, created erosion by cutting and burning forests on mountain slopes, and allowed livestock to overgraze the land. These actions created a habitat unfit not only for mountain lions, bears, and wolves, but also for people. Today, many of our activities are seriously affecting the quality of the air, water, and land that we all share. Too many humans are using up too much of the earth's resources.*

However, with our intelligence, compassion, and energy, we can be a wonderful, even magical people. We can identify problems, find solutions, and put those solutions to work. For example, a well-thought-out action such as recycling can have positive effects. Less land is disturbed in digging up minerals and containing garbage. Both energy and habitat are saved.

In the puppet show "The Animals' Court," the main character, Mrs. Ava Rice, learns that her actions have had serious consequences for the planet. However, Mrs. Ava Rice represents not only the worst in us, but also the best.

The Animals' Court
(A Puppet Play)

CHARACTERS:
NARRATOR
MRS. AVA RICE
JUDGE (lion)
PROSECUTING ATTORNEY (snowy owl)
DEFENSE ATTORNEY (cockroach)
WITNESSES:
      FLORIDA PANTHER
      RED-TAILED PARROT
      SNOW LEOPARD
      AMERICAN BISON

NARRATOR — Mrs. Ava Rice was a greedy, selfish, and wasteful woman. She was *all* the time what you and I are only sometimes. She surrounded herself with "things" that she tired of very quickly. Her closets were crammed with coats, shoes, and handbags made from the furs and skins of many wild animals. Her jewelry box overflowed with ivory earrings, necklaces, and bracelets. She never wore these things more than once. She said that she loved animals. Didn't she have beautiful parrots straight from the jungles of South America?

She never recycled her diet pop cans, newspapers, or glass bottles. She didn't have time! She drove her car, even if she was going only across the street. She had the money for gas, why should she walk? She never visited zoos (they were noisy and smelly!) or museums (boring!) to learn about the creatures with whom she shared the planet. Even though she lived in an area where water was scarce, she let the faucet run while she brushed her teeth. She over-watered her lawn and washed her car whether it needed it or not. After all, she thought water was for people — not for alligators or panthers.

One evening, a young man told her politely that because she did not move with the grace and strength of the snow leopard, the fur's beauty was lost on her. Disturbed, she went home quite early, and went to bed. That night she had a dream that changed her life.

THE DREAM

JUDGE (lion) — Order in the court! The defendant is present. Let the proceedings begin.

PROSECUTING ATTORNEY (snowy owl) — We are assembled today to judge the guilt or innocence of Mrs. Ava Rice and other members of her species (*Homo sapiens*) concerning crimes committed against earth and its inhabitants.

I'm ready to call my first witness.

(To her credit Mrs. Ava Rice speaks up.)

MRS. AVA RICE (*Homo sapiens*) — But I deserve a defense. I have the right to a lawyer. It's in the Constitution (isn't it?) or the Bill of Rights, well, one of those!

(The animals confer.)

JUDGE — Cockroach will represent you. He's been on the earth for quite a long time. He's knowledgeable, and holds no grudge against humans. Says he's doing quite well himself.

(Cockroach wiggles his long antennae at Mrs. Ava Rice.)

MRS. AVA RICE — Oh my! But if you're all there is, I guess you'll have to do.

JUDGE — First witness, please.

PROSECUTING ATTORNEY — The prosecution calls Florida panther.

(Florida panther walks to the stand.)

PROSECUTING ATTORNEY — For the benefit of the court, state your scientific name and address.

PANTHER — Florida panther, *Felis concolor coryi*, south Florida.

PROSECUTING ATTORNEY — And what is your complaint against the defendant?

PANTHER — I am one of the most endangered mammals in the world. Only 30 of my kind survive in the tree islands and grassy waters of south Florida. Our persecution began a long time ago. Fearing for their lives and their cows, early settlers destroyed us every chance they got. They even put a price on our heads — $5.00 per scalp.

COCKROACH *(adjusting his sunglasses)* — Forgive the shades, Your Honor, but the bright lights of the courtroom hurt my eyes. Members of my species prefer the dark.

JUDGE *(clearing his throat)* — Proceed, Cockroach.

COCKROACH — My argument is simple. Is it fair to blame humans if your species is in trouble? Regard the roach! There are some 3,500 species of cockroaches, and we live all over the world. Cockroaches are survivors. They are flexible and adaptable. My advice to you, Panther, is to follow the wisdom of a superior species, the cockroach. In other words, lighten up! Chill out! Go with the flow!

(The cockroach waves his antennae at Mrs. Ava Rice.)

By the way Ava, my fee is quite reasonable. I understand that you live in Florida, a favorite retirement spot for those of my kind. What do you say to room and board for myself and my relatives? Currently, 99,999 of us are living in a four-room apartment in Texas. It's very crowded, and…*

(Mrs. Ava Rice shudders.)

JUDGE — Cockroach, keep your comments brief and to the point. Proceed with your testimony, Panther.

In 1947, roach researchers surveying a four-room apartment in Austin, Texas, estimated that between 50,000 and 100,000 cockroaches lived there.

PANTHER — *(disgusted)* Unlike the cockroach, we are so rare today, humans are not permitted to shoot us — but they do. Farm fields, houses, and factories gobble up the land. Roads crisscross the grassy plains and bring humans to our secret places. Crossing these roads, panthers are hit and killed.

Once the fresh, sweet water flowed gently over our land. But humans built canals and flood gates and straightened the river. Now the land is either too dry or too wet. Deer drown when the land floods, and wood storks cannot find enough food to raise their young. Humans are taking more than the land is able to give.

JUDGE — Thank you, Florida Panther. You may step down. Next witness, please.

(The red-tailed parrot flies to the witness stand.)

PARROT — I am the red-tailed parrot, *Amazona brasiliensis*. My home in the jungle of Brazil has grown smaller and smaller. Humans cleared the forest, and trapped many parrots. Forced into tiny cages and given little food or water, many birds died. Our beaks were taped and our wings bound to our bodies. We were shipped in closed dark boxes to strange places. Many more parrots died. People bought us and took us "home. . ."

COCKROACH — But, Parrot, from the condition of your feathers, you look "none the worse for wear." No, *Amazona*, it is not the human species that brings your downfall, it is your pride! A toast to the roach! Are we too proud to eat a crust of bread that has fallen to the floor? A cockroach makes a feast from another's garbage. And you, *Amazona*, fed the finest foods, live like a queen, safe within your gilded cage.

PARROT *(feathers ruffled)* — And the rest of my life I will view the world through the bars of that cage. My humans love me. But if they knew the suffering, perhaps they would buy only birds that had been bred and raised to be pets. For every wild parrot they buy, many wild birds have died.

(The beautiful parrot flies from the stand.)

JUDGE — Next witness.

(The snow leopard gracefully leaps to the stand.)

SNOW LEOPARD — I am the snow leopard, *Panthera uncia*. I live on the rocky slopes of high, cold mountains. My kind is very rare.

I speak for all animals who are killed for their fur, their skin, or their tusks. Is a picture of an elephant carved on its own ivory tusk more valuable than the great creature itself? Is a zebra's skin more handsome on a wall than on itself? Do the stripes of the tiger not belong to the tiger? Even when humans make laws to protect us, poachers will kill us because you will pay. Let the tiger keep his stripes and the snow leopard her spots.

(Mrs. Ava Rice looks down.)

COCKROACH *(slowly shaking his head)* — Ah, *Panthera, Panthera*, celebrate the cockroach! Again, I must humbly demonstrate the superiority of my species. Cockroaches have lived on this earth for 250 million years, and in that time have changed very little. We have survived war, famine, flood, and insecticides. Wherever there are humans in the world, we are there to keep them company — in their grocery stores, restaurants, bakeries, and kitchen cupboards. In fact, if my human friends continue to treat the planet as they have in the past, the earth will one day belong only to cockroaches and humans.

(Cockroach fondly touches Mrs. Ava Rice's shoulder with his long, bristly leg.)

(Mrs. Ava Rice screams and slaps at the bristly leg resting on her shoulder.)

COCKROACH *(surprised)* — Well, that's gratitude for you! As you appear to have no respect for my professional integrity, I will take my leave.

(Cockroach gathers up materials.)

No hard feelings, I can afford to be generous — the roach has a rosy future. Your home is my home, *Homo sapiens!*

(Chuckling, Cockroach leaves the courtroom.)

JUDGE *(hitting his gavel)* — Order, order in the court *(he roars)*! Next and last witness, please.

(The American bison lumbers to the stand.)

BISON — I am the American bison, *Bison bison.* I speak partly in defense of humans. Once millions of us roamed the great plains, and millions of us were slaughtered. At one time there were less than 1,000 of us left. Now we are over 80,000 strong. Humans brought us back from the edge. People are helping the whooping crane, American alligator, giant panda, and the trumpeter swan. Your Honor, these humans do some good.

JUDGE — Mrs. Ava Rice, do you have anything to say in your behalf?

(Mrs. Ava Rice shakes her head.)

JUDGE — Mrs. Ava Rice, rise and face your wild brothers and sisters.

(Mrs. Ava Rice rises and faces the Florida panther, the red-tailed parrot, the snow leopard, the bison, and other assembled wild creatures.)

JUDGE — Your greatest crimes are ignorance and thoughtlessness. Whatever you do affects the earth and all of us. Members of your species are powerful creatures. Everything you do makes a difference.

If humans choose to protect the earth, your home and ours, we all benefit. But if avarice, ignorance, and selfishness guide your actions, this court will not punish you. You will punish yourselves.

NARRATOR — Mrs. Ava Rice awoke with a start. From that dream on, she was a different person. Everyone marveled at the change in her. A few of her friends even followed her example.

She never wore another fur coat — she chose cotton or wool instead. She conserved water and gasoline and recycled her cans, glass, and paper. She became involved in organizations that protected animals and their habitat.

However, she kept the snow leopard coat — not because she wanted to wear it, but to remind herself that the snow leopard never would.

THE END.

(Applause — lots of it!)

Write your own puppet script!

Teach your classmates and parents about endangered animals and the threat of extinction. Or, create a story that tells adults and kids how they can be more responsible members of the earth family. Use the puppets from "The Animals' Court," or design your own.

If you would like to involve more people in your show, design animal masks from paper bags, and be puppets yourselves!

Lion hunt

"IT'S A FRESH TRACK, KERRY. It couldn't be more than an hour old."

The young, dark-haired man bent over the print. It was on top of the fresh snow. The edge of the track was sharp, not rounded as a result of the wind blowing over it for days. He felt the track; it was soft and pliable, not frozen.

"O.K., let's put the hounds on it," he said. The dogs were anxious; this was their work and they loved it! "Calm down, Sally. You find that cat, Abbey. All right, Hatchet, have at it!" The young man watched as his dogs, noses to the ground and tails wagging excitedly, began running the line of scent left behind by the lion in its tracks. He smiled slightly. He sure missed Spook. Spook had been his first hound, and although it usually took two to three years to train a good cat dog, it had taken only six months for Spook. Spook was retired now. The old dog had earned the right to sleep in the sun.

Packing their 35 pounds (16 kilograms) of gear, Kerry and Greg followed the dogs on foot. It was a cold, crisp December morning. With the sun up the temperature was climbing from the early morning low of -10 degrees F (-23 degrees C).

The men had been walking for about an hour. Suddenly they stopped and listened. The hounds' baying had changed. Kerry turned to Greg. "Sounds like they've got her in a tree."

When the two men arrived on the scene, the three dogs were barking excitedly at the base of a large fir tree. Greg secured the dogs and Kerry removed a gun from his pack and assembled it. He loaded it, and, moving around the base of the tree, positioned himself for a good shot at the lion. He preferred a rump shot, but he could put it in the shoulder if he had to. He aimed and fired. It was a hit! However, this lion would not find itself mounted as someone's trophy.

Kerry Murphy and Greg Felzien are research biologists. The lion, subdued with a tranquilizing dart, is part of an ongoing five-year study of mountain lions in Yellowstone National Park. Yellowstone National Park is located in the northwest corner of Wyoming. The lion study is being conducted on the northern range (see the map on page 50). In winter, lions prefer the lower elevation of this northern section with its lighter snow pack. Conditions are much more severe in the interior of the park.

A mountain lion has five toes on each of its front feet. The dewclaw is located above the paw on the inside of the front legs and does not show in the track. The back paws each have four toes.

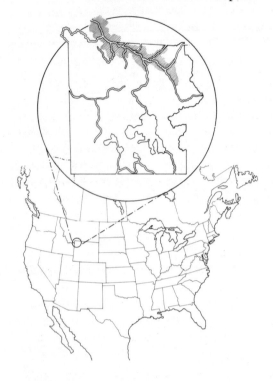

Mountain lion study
area in Yellowstone park.

*A mountain lion's
front claws are
about one inch (2.5
centimeters) long.*

THE STUDY IN YELLOWSTONE

was initiated by Dr. Maurice Hornocker (see "The Man Who Loves Mountain Lions"). Dr. Hornocker and researcher Gary Koehler surveyed Yellowstone National Park in 1986 to determine if lions still lived there. During the late 1800s and early 1900s, mountain lions (as well as wolves and coyotes) were killed in the park and throughout the West. Wildlife managers believed that eliminating predators (the "bad animals") was a way to protect elk, deer, and livestock (the "good animals"). By 1930, wolves and mountain lions left no tracks in Yellowstone.

However, from his brief survey, Dr. Hornocker speculated that there were mountain lions living in Yellowstone National Park. To know for sure, more research was needed.

Under Dr. Hornocker's direction, Kerry Murphy began his study of Yellowstone's lions in the fall of 1987. Kerry's first objective was to fit as many lions as possible with radio collars. These lions would not be able to listen to their favorite rap tunes. But researchers would be able to follow their movements with an antenna that would pick up the signal transmitted by the radio collar. Over 50 lions in the Yellowstone study area have these collars.

As soon as the lion is darted and subdued, Kerry or Greg must climb the tree to ensure that the lion is not so drugged that it will crash to the ground. Safety is always a concern. Using a system of ropes, they gently lower the animal out of the tree.

Once the lion is on the ground the researchers work quickly — they have about 30 minutes before the drug wears off. Because of their concern for the animal, they will not administer a second dose.

The cat's vital signs are checked. Eye ointment is applied (the drug tends to dry the eyes). The age and sex of the lion are recorded. This information is very important; the collar must be fitted to the growth potential of the animal. The radio collar is put on and tested. The cat's ears are tattooed and ear tags are attached. The number on these tags is visible to a researcher with binoculars, or to a hunter who has treed the cat. However, there is no law against killing tagged lions.

The mountain lion is weighed and measured. A vial of blood is removed for study. Eye color and the overall condition of the cat are recorded.

In North America, male mountain lions weigh 120 to 165 pounds (54 to 75 kilograms). Females usually weigh less, between 80 and 100 pounds (36 to 45 kilograms).

One very large mountain lion tipped the scales at 300 pounds (136 kilograms)!

Their examination complete, Kerry and Greg remain in the area and observe the lion as the drug wears off. They will not leave until they are certain that the animal can move about and defend itself.

From their work, these researchers hope to discover the size of the mountain lion population in Yellowstone and whether it is increasing or decreasing. They hope to determine when and what the lion eats, how it kills, how often it kills, and how completely it uses its prey. By observing lion kills, they hope to discover the cat's relationship with other predators or scavengers. (What animals benefit by eating the mountain lion's left-overs? What animals might chase a lion from its own kill?)

Kittens of all females in the study area also are fitted with "expandable" radio collars that will grow with the young cat. From tracking the signals of these kittens, researchers are able to find out what happens to them. Kerry and his team have found that many of the kittens die. Other predators eat them. Sometimes they are orphaned because hunters kill the mother or the mother dies of natural causes.

Mountain lion research is being conducted in many areas throughout the country, including Arizona, Colorado, Idaho, New Mexico, and Florida. Although adapted to their particular needs and study areas, the techniques used by Kerry and his team are common among lion researchers.

Thanks to Kerry and his hounds, we have an opportunity to share the secrets of the lions of Yellowstone. And with managers throughout the country armed with the knowledge to make more enlightened decisions, the mountain lion can look to a brighter future.

The Man Who Loves Mountain *lions*

DR. MAURICE HORNOCKER has studied grizzly bears in Yellowstone National Park, jaguars in Brazil, leopards in Africa, Siberian tigers in Russia, and mountain lions throughout their range in North and South America. He is recognized throughout the world for his work with predators. However, when Maurice was nine years old cleaning out stables and feeding hogs and horses on a small family farm in Iowa, he could not have known where his love of animals and the outdoor life would lead him.

As a boy, Maurice hunted and fished. He attended a one-room school. Resources were limited in the small, rural community. When the bookmobile made its monthly visit, Maurice eagerly searched the shelves for books about birds and mammals.

Maurice was a good student. He won the county spelling bee and was valedictorian of his high school class. He tried out for and made the basketball team, but the coach had to convince the boy's father to allow Maurice to play. Throughout his early years, Maurice was torn between his school and career interests and his strong German father who insisted Maurice "make a living" from the family farm.

Because of the Korean Conflict, Maurice joined the navy after high school and worked in submarines. His world was broadened by new people and experiences. He discovered there was a place in it for those who shared his curiosity and love for wilderness — wildlife biology.

Discharged from the navy in 1951, Maurice returned to the family farm. A series of events strengthened Maurice's resolve to pursue a career in wildlife research. In September 1955, he enrolled at the University of Montana.

There Maurice came under the influence of biologist John Craighead, now recognized worldwide for his contribution to wildlife science. Dr. Craighead told the young graduate student, "This work is a way of life, not a job. It is something you do because you love it. It is a labor of love."

Maurice worked on a number of projects with Dr. Craighead — from magpies to the grizzly bears of Yellowstone National Park. As he watched his assistant grow in knowledge and experience, Dr. Craighead knew that it was time for Maurice to have his own project. In 1963, Maurice began his work with mountain lions.

Dr. Maurice Hornocker (born 1930)

A mountain lion can eat about 10 pounds (4.5 kilograms) of meat at one time. That amount is about the same as 100 hotdogs!

Dr. Hornocker recalls the anxiety he felt about this first lion project: "We didn't know if we could catch lions or mark them. We didn't know once we did mark them if we would ever see them again. There were so many unknowns, so many chances for failure. It was an enormous risk. . . I kept asking myself, 'How will I ever do it?' "

Although Dr. Hornocker began his work with mountain lions in Montana, the project was moved to Idaho. At the time of the study, mountain lions were considered "vermin." They were shot at every opportunity. Within the first year, 9 of the 14 originally collared lions were shot in Montana. A more isolated area for study was required.

Dr. Hornocker moved his project to the rugged wilderness of Idaho. For 10 years, Maurice Hornocker and his assistants studied a population of mountain lions in the River of No Return Wilderness in central Idaho. The results of their work provided a base for all mountain lion research that would follow in other parts of the country. In 1984, researchers returned to the same study area to "check" their original findings. The result? Their original conclusions were correct.

Today, Dr. Hornocker is the director of the Wildlife Research Institute in Moscow, Idaho. He and his team of researchers study mountain lions, bobcats, lynx, leopards, coyotes, whooping cranes, and a number of rare, threatened, and endangered birds and mammals.

Beyond the scientific data, Maurice Hornocker's achievements carry a personal message. Each of us must pay attention to the dreams and talents that live within us. Parents, teachers, and children must foster and encourage these interests in each other. Because a single person, responding to a love that burns within, can accomplish great things.

A mountain lion lazily switches its long tail as it views the canyon below from its rocky ledge. In part, this lion survives because of a man who loves mountain lions.

The Range game

THE RANGE OF

Felis concolor once extended from the Atlantic to the Pacific Ocean and from northern Canada to the tip of South America. With the arrival of the Europeans, the lion was hunted, trapped, and poisoned. As early as the late 1600s, eastern colonies were offering bounties for killing lions. (A bounty is money paid for the killing of an animal.) As settlers moved westward, bounties for the control of the lion spread with them.

During the early 1900s, there was a national program to wipe out predators. In addition to mountain lions, wolves and coyotes were killed, even in national parks. As people learned more about the value of predators, they began to realize that mountain lions, wolves, coyotes, and animals like them had important jobs in nature. But it was too late for the eastern lion.

TODAY IN NORTH AMERICA,

mountain lions are found from the Rocky Mountains to the Pacific coast. They have disappeared from the central United States. Lions are occasionally seen in the East, but the only recognized eastern population is in southern Florida, the endangered Florida panther. Although mountain lions have been eliminated in many areas, the animal is still common in parts of Mexico and Central America. It is scattered throughout South America.

Find the lions!

Carefully study the map on the next page. Find the hidden mountain lions. (Hint: There are 15.)

To help you in your search, consider the following questions:

1. What does a mountain lion need to live? A condominium? A shopping mall? Or fresh water, clean air, food, and cover such as forests and rugged, undeveloped mountains? If a mountain lion needs water, food, and cover, then search for the cat in regions that provide these things.

2. What animals share the same habitat as mountain lions? Why? Do these animals share the mountain lion's need for fresh water, clean air, food, and cover?

3. Why do deer and mountain lions often inhabit the same area?

4. Locate the area where you live. Except in zoos, do mountain lions live close to you?

5. In what parts of the United States are mountain lions and people sharing habitat? Can mountain lions and people live together? (See "Living with *León*", page 56.)

Mountain lions once lived almost everywhere in the United States. Imagine that you are an artist living in the early days of our country. On a separate sheet of paper, trace the outline of the map on the next page. On the map illustrate how the United States might have looked about 250 years ago. (Reference books will be very useful.)

Living with león

STUDENTS LIVING IN A *housing complex at the University of Montana are warned to monitor children and pets more closely. A mountain lion has been seen in the area.*

In Boulder County, Colorado, a jogger is treed by two mountain lions. The woman eventually escapes unharmed.

In a neighborhood of Colorado Springs, Colorado, three dogs are killed by a mountain lion in one year. After the third killing, the lion is found resting under a resident's porch. Colorado Division of Wildlife officers tranquilize and move the lion to a wilderness area.

An 18-year-old, jogging on the mountain slope behind his school in Idaho Springs, Colorado, is killed by a mountain lion. In the past 100 years, he is the second adult to be killed by a mountain lion in all of Canada and the western United States.

IN AREAS SUCH AS BOULDER, Colorado; Missoula, Montana; and other urban centers of Arizona, New Mexico, and California, people and mountain lion encounters are on the increase. Most often the experience of seeing a mountain lion in the wild is similar to the feelings we have when receiving a gift — surprise, excitement, and wonder. In *"El Encanto,"* María and Don Miguel shared these feelings in their meeting with the mountain lion. However, contact between lions and people sometimes results in conflict.

As people move from towns and cities, and build mountain homes and recreational cabins, they are settling in mountain lion habitat. Mountain lions are territorial. Experienced lions maintain choice, isolated territories, and younger lions, seeking to establish territories, are getting the left-overs — areas where people are abundant and food and cover are reduced. These inexperienced hunters may be more likely to take prey such as dogs and cats. But, all lions are opportunistic and will take an "easy meal" when it is available. In some areas where mountain lions and people share habitat, the lions are becoming accustomed to humans. As a result, the cats are bolder in their encounters with humans.

Deer populations are high in these areas. Deer feed on manicured lawns, in gardens, and on landscaped shopping mall plazas. Mountain lions stalking deer in these areas are encountering dogs, cats, joggers, and children.

Most people agree that they would like to live with *león*, but they also need to feel safe. How can we live or play in or close to mountain lion country and still maintain some level of comfort and security?

Hiking or living in or near wilderness requires a person to accept responsibility for the experience. Every activity we participate in involves risk. We accept the responsibility of driving a car by studying and following the rules of the road. We reduce our risk by wearing a safety belt.

Responsible wilderness residents or hikers learn as much as they can about the mountain lion and its behavior. They learn to identify the signs of the lion such as tracks, scat, scrapes, kills, and claw marks.

Residents educate their children about wilderness living. At night, pets are brought indoors and livestock is secured.

Hikers travel in groups, on horseback, or with one or more aggressive dogs to reduce their risk. (Be sure that dogs are permitted on trails.) Children stay with their parents, and never hike alone — particularly not in lion country. Backcountry visitors make noise so that a mountain lion or other wild animal is not taken by surprise. Although lions are rarely surprised by humans due to their keen senses, if you do surprise a lion, the noise will give the animal the time and space needed to escape.

If you encounter a lion, assume a neutral posture and do not make eye contact. Do not crouch, turn your back, or run away from the mountain lion. The responsible individual recognizes that a lion feeding on a carcass or a mother with young can be very dangerous.

This information has been provided for the same reason that you have fire drills at school. There will probably never be a fire in your school. However, being prepared for the possibility may prevent you from panicking — a condition that would reduce your chances of escape. In the unlikely event that an individual is attacked by a lion, he or she should scream and wave his or her arms above the head to confuse the animal. One researcher suggested raising above the head any object that increases body bulk and height. He reported that even the big cats appear afraid of large objects approaching quickly, especially from above.

Another scientist indicated that mountain lions have been driven away from victims either by the victim acting aggressively (one trainer attacked inside a lion's cage punched and kicked it) or by other people running, yelling, and hitting at the lion with sticks about its head. If the attack ensues, the victim must protect his or her head and neck by covering them with the arms.

Most mountain lions avoid contact with humans. However, report to a wildlife officer any unusual lion behavior or an attack.

This information is neither complete nor foolproof. Mountain lions have different personalities. What works with one lion may not work with another. If you live or hike in lion country, be alert, stay informed about new research findings, and learn all you can about this fascinating cat.

In the wild, a mountain lion 8 to 12 years of age is considered old.

Tracking the *cat*

THROUGHOUT THIS book you have been following the mountain lion's "fact tracks." Let's see how good a tracker you have become. You have been hired to study mountain lions in a wilderness area close to a large city. Your plan is to capture and radio-collar lions to learn more about their habits and movements. To find the mountain lion in the maze, follow the open path until you come to a cat track. Within the cat track, you will find a "challenge." Select the right answer and follow the path on which the answer is found. If your selection leads you to a dead end, back track to the question and try again. Sometimes there will be more than one right path.

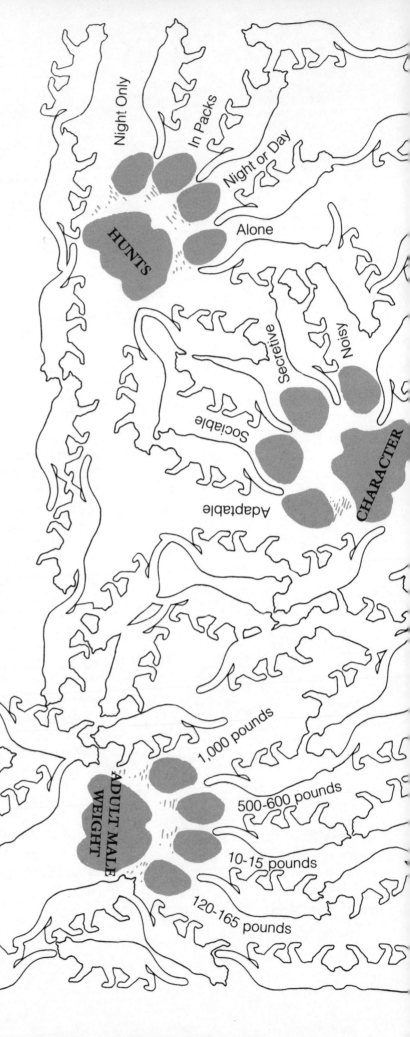

HUNTS

Night Only

In Packs

Night or Day

Alone

CHARACTER

Secretive

Noisy

Sociable

Adaptable

ADULT MALE WEIGHT

1,000 pounds

500-600 pounds

10-15 pounds

120-165 pounds

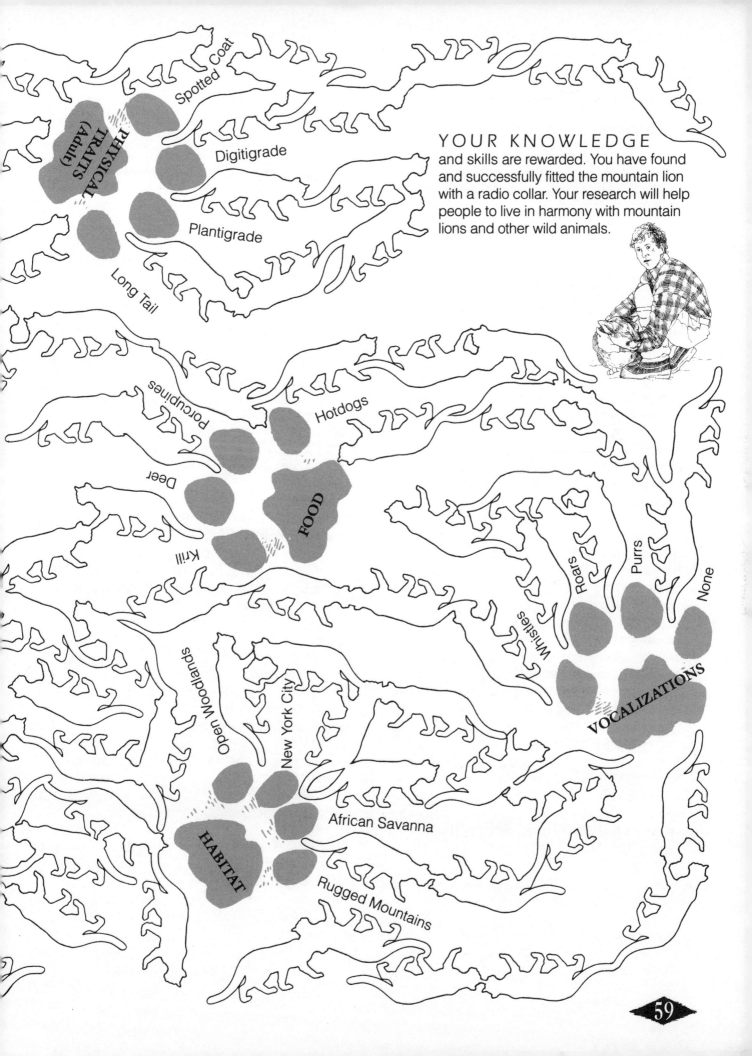

PHYSICAL TRAITS (Adult)
Spotted Coat
Digitigrade
Plantigrade
Long Tail

YOUR KNOWLEDGE
and skills are rewarded. You have found and successfully fitted the mountain lion with a radio collar. Your research will help people to live in harmony with mountain lions and other wild animals.

FOOD
Porcupines
Hotdogs
Deer
Krill

VOCALIZATIONS
Roars
Purrs
None
Whistles

HABITAT
Open Woodlands
New York City
African Savanna
Rugged Mountains

Glossary

adobe house (uh-DOH-bee house) — A house made with sun-dried bricks of clay. These houses are common in Mexico and the American Southwest. Traditional adobe houses are covered with mud.

Ava Rice (Mrs.) (AV-uh-ruhs) — (avarice) This term describes an individual who is greedy and seeks to accumulate great wealth.

bounty (BOWNT-ee) — An amount of money paid to a hunter for killing predators such as mountain lions, coyotes, and wolves.

carcass (CAHR-cuhs) — The body of a dead animal.

carnivore (cahr-NIH-vohr) — An animal whose diet is made up almost completely of meat. Carnivores such as mountain lions belong to the order Carnivora.

cheek teeth (CHEEK-TEETH) — The premolars and molars found in the cheek area of the mouth.

common name (KAHM-uhn NAYM) — The name that an animal is given by people in a particular region or time period. The same animal may have many different common names, and different animals may have the same common name.

curandera (koo-ran-DEH-rah) — (or "curer") Many rural Mexican communities had no doctors. Instead, a woman who was familiar with herbs and medicinal plants would be called to the bedside of a sick person or a woman in childbirth. The *curandera* was often considered a "wise woman."

dewclaw (DOO-klaw) — The fifth toe on the front foot of certain members of the cat (and dog) family. The dewclaw is located on the inside of the front legs above the paw.

digitigrade (DIHJ-uht-uh-grayd) — To walk or run on the digits or toes of the foot.

don (DAHN) — A title used out of courtesy and respect for Spanish men, used only with the Christian name.

doña (DOH-nyeh) — A title used out of courtesy and respect for Spanish women, used only with the Christian name.

dung heap (DUHNG heep) — A pile of scat. A mountain lion buries dung heaps in the area of a carcass on which the animal has been feeding.

esophagus (ih-SAHF-uh-guhs) — The tube through which food passes from the pharynx to the stomach.

habitat (HAB-uh-tat) — The area in which an animal lives. Good habitat provides an animal with clean air, water, food, and cover.

home range (HOHM-raynj) — The area where a mountain lion rests, hunts, and finds mates. The size of the home range varies with the age, sex, and reproductive stage of the mountain lion. A female with young kittens has a smaller range than one with older kittens that require more food. The season of the year and the distribution and density of prey also affect the size of the home range.

león (LAY-ohn) — The term Spanish-Americans and Mexicans use when referring to the mountain lion.

metate (meh-TAHT-ee) — A stone used for grinding corn and other grains.

mortality (mohr-TAL-eht-ee) — Death rate.

opportunistic (ahp-ohr-TOO-nihs-tihk) — Taking advantage of an "opportunity" (a situation that favors you). For example, although mountain lions generally hunt at night, they are opportunistic because they also will hunt during the day if prey is available.

padrino (pah-DREE-no) — Godfather, sponsor.

plantigrade (PLANT-uh-grayd) — Walking on the entire sole or bottom of the feet.

prey (PRAY) — Any animal that is hunted and fed upon by another animal.

retractable claws (rih-TRAK-teh-behl KLAWZ) — Muscles that are attached to a cat's claws allow the animal to withdraw its claws into pockets in its feet and to extend them when needed (climbing, killing prey, etc.). Most cats have retractable claws; one exception is the cheetah.

scat (SKAT) — The fecal matter or droppings of mammals.

scientific name (seye-uhn-TIF-ik NAYM) — Derived from a naming system developed by Carolus Linnaeus. A scientific name has two parts, and the words are usually from Latin or Greek languages. Every known plant or animal has only one correct scientific name.

scrape (SKRAYP) (or scratch) — Mounds of dirt, twigs, and grass that mountain lions and other cats make by scratching the dirt with their feet.

señora (see-NYOHR-eh) — The Spanish title for a married woman (like "Mrs." in English).

tapetum (teh-PEET-ehm) — A mirror-like structure at the back of a cat's eye that provides the animal with good night vision. At night when you shine light into a cat's eyes, the animal's eyes will glow. This "eyeshine" occurs because of the reflective properties of the tapetum.

tawny (TAW-nee) — A color ranging from light brown to yellowish-brown. The coat of the mountain lion is most often described as "tawny."

tortillas (tawr-TEE-yehz) — Made of corn meal or flour, this food is shaped like a flat, thin pancake. Tortillas were originally used like silverware to scoop up beans and rice. They are commonly eaten in Mexico and throughout the American Southwest.

Bibliography

Ballesteros, Octavio A. 1979. *Mexican Proverbs*. Eakin Press, Austin, Texas.

Chapman, Joseph A. 1983. *Wild Mammals of North America*. Johns Hopkins University Press, Baltimore.

Gray, Robert. 1972. *Cougar*. Grosset and Dunlap, New York.*

Halfpenny, James. 1986. *Field Guide to Mammal Tracking in Western America*. Johnson Books, Boulder, Colorado.

Hornocker, Maurice G. March 1970. "An Analysis of Mountain Lion Predation upon Mule Deer and Elk in the Idaho Primitive Area," in *Wildlife Monographs*. The Wildlife Society, Washington, D.C.

Leopold, Starker A. 1959. *Wildlife of Mexico*. University of California Press, Berkeley, California.

Line, Les. 1985. *The Audubon Society Book of Wild Cats*. Harry N. Abrams, Inc., Publishers, New York.

Parsons, Alexandra. 1990. *Amazing Cats*. Alfred A. Knopf, New York.*

Robinson, William L. 1989. *Wildlife Ecology and Management*. Macmillan Publishing Company, New York.

Schmidt, John L., and Douglas L. Gilbert. 1978. *Big Game of North America*. Stackpole Books, Harrisburg, Pennsylvania.

Smith, Ronald H. (ed.) 1989. *Proceedings of the Third Mountain Lion Workshop*. Arizona Chapter, The Wildlife Society and Arizona Game and Fish Department, Arizona.

Springer, Kim (ed.). 1987. *Looking at the American Lion*. Biologue, Vol. 2, Number 1, Teton Science School, Kelly, Wyoming.*

Tinsley, Jim Bob. 1987. *The Puma, Legendary Lion of the Americas*. Texas Western Press, El Paso.

Wexco, John Bonnett. 1988. *Little Cats: Zoobooks, Vol. 6, #1*. Wildlife Education, Ltd., San Diego, California.*

Wexco, John Bonnett. 1987. *Endangered Animals: Zoobooks, Vol. 4, #8*. Wildlife Education, Ltd., San Diego, California.*

Young, Stanley P., and Edward A. Goldman. 1964. *The Puma, Mysterious American Cat*. Dover Publications, Inc., New York.

Interviews with mountain lion researcher Kerry Murphy, Yellowstone National Park, October 1990.

Interview with Dr. Maurice Hornocker, Gardiner, Montana, December 1990.

*Books of interest for younger readers

Key

Cat of Many Names Puzzle (page 27)

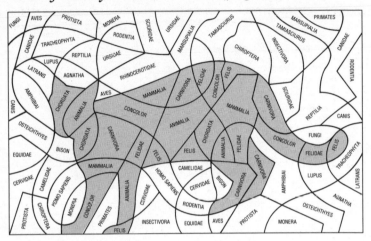

Sign of the Lion Picture (page 42)

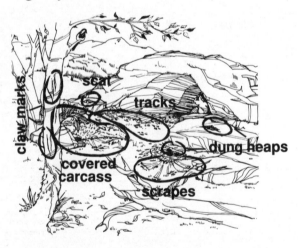

The Range Game Map (page 55)

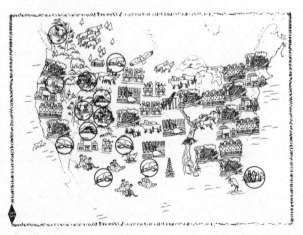

The Denver Museum of Natural History appreciates the encouragement, time, and support of the following individuals:

Project Sponsor — Valerie Gates Harbaugh

Publication Coordinator — Betsy R. Armstrong

Technical Review — Dr. David Carrasco, University of Colorado; Bob Hernbrode, Colorado Division of Wildlife; Dr. Maurice Hornocker, Wildlife Research Institute; Rick LoBello, Big Bend National Park; Dr. Marianne Stoller, Colorado College

The Museum's Technical and Educational Team — Diana Crew, Manager of Project Development; Michelle Conger, Natural Sciences Educator; Dr. Jane Day, Chief Curator; Thielma Gamewell, Museum Shop; Joyce Herold, Curator of Ethnography; Dr. Carron Meaney, Curator of Mammalogy; Karen Nein, Editor

Design — Ann W. Douden, Gail Kohler Opsahl
Cover Illustration — Ann W. Douden

Illustrations — Ann W. Douden, Gail Kohler Opsahl, Marjorie C. Leggitt, Roberta Caldwell, Marcia McGivern, Roberta Shupe

Production — J. Keith Abernathy, Danielle B. Okin

Thanks also to the kids, moms, and granddads who tested the activities.

Design motifs: traditional serape design from Saltillo, Mexico, from the Crane American Indian Collection, Denver Museum of Natural History..

Tracking the Cat Maze (pages 58-59)

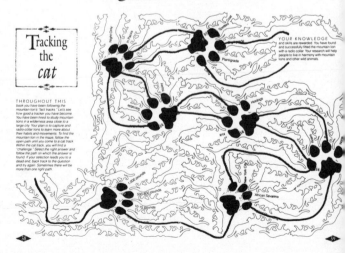